W9-BNQ-240

DARK HARBOR

DARK HARBOR

THE WAR FOR THE
NEW YORK WATERFRONT

NATHAN WARD

FARRAR, STRAUS AND GIROUX   NEW YORK

Farrar, Straus and Giroux
18 West 18th Street, New York 10011

Copyright © 2010 by Nathan Ward
Map copyright © 2010 by Jeffrey L. Ward
All rights reserved
Distributed in Canada by D&M Publishers, Inc.
Printed in the United States of America
First edition, 2010

Library of Congress Cataloging-in-Publication Data
Ward, Nathan, 1963–
    Dark harbor : the war for the New York waterfront / Nathan Ward.— 1st ed.
    p.   cm.
    ISBN 978-0-374-28622-4 (hbk. : alk. paper)
    1. Organized crime—New York (State)—New York—Case studies   2. Stevedores—
Labor unions—New York (State)—New York—Case studies.   3. Labor unions—
Corrupt practices—New York (State)—New York—Case studies.   4. Murder—New
York (State)—New York—Case studies.   5. Johnson, Malcolm M. (Malcolm Malone),
1904–1976.   I. Title.

HV6452.N7W37 2010
364.1'06609747—dc22

                                                                    2009045680

Designed by Abby Kagan

www.fsgbooks.com

10   9   8   7   6   5   4   3   2   1

FOR MY FAMILY,
FOR NICHOLAS AND NINA,
AND FOR KATIE, ALWAYS

J'accuse—yes, I accuse—but it's not merely a petty criminal I am accusing . . . He would be powerless without support, and the support which he has been given by certain police officers, magistrates, and lawyers gives him good reason to believe that he can obtain any impunity he may need.

—GRAHAM GREENE, *J'Accuse*

CONTENTS

CONTENTS

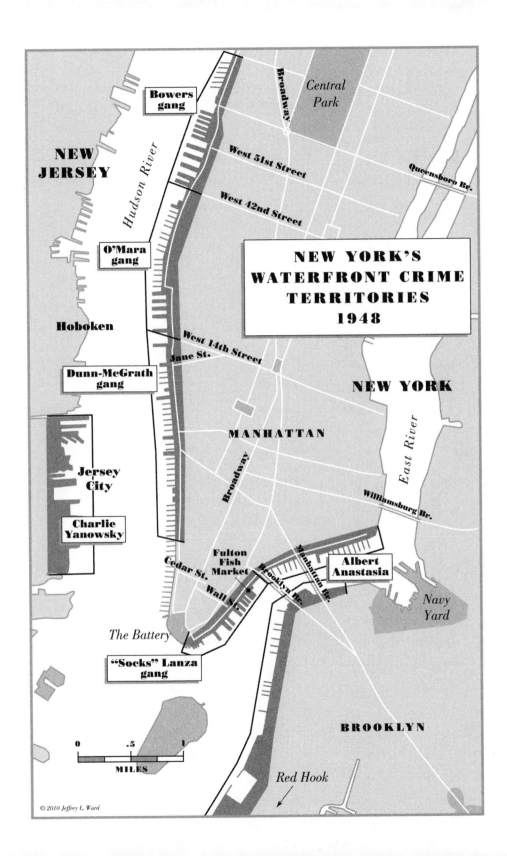

PREFACE: WHO WANTS TO BE A DEAD HERO?

"Oh, I know what you want to hear about," Jim Longhi said with false reluctance the first time I called him, interrupting a chess game with his wife, Gabrielle. "The old waterfront—gangsters, rackets, the Anastasias."

He was right. My interest in what Mr. Longhi elegantly called the "criminal coloration" of the docks was what had brought us together. Longhi was a cultured Manhattan attorney on the threshold of his nineties when we met in his cheerful apartment on Sutton Place one summer afternoon. He had just removed his work tie from the collar of his silk shirt as he led me out onto his small balcony. Below us and a few hundred yards away was the East River, a pretty staid thoroughfare at that point in its life compared to the rough old waterfront I had come to hear about, and Mr. Longhi weighed the calm barge traffic he saw against the river in his head. "A very different waterfront," he judged. As we talked about his early days, the suave manners of the Columbia-educated attorney loosened a bit, following his tie, revealing a son of the Brooklyn docks. Longhi's father had been a radical docks organizer ("When I was born, my father had seven bodyguards, seven Italians with ice picks!"), and he had started out himself as a waterfront lawyer like Mr. Alfieri, the character his friend Arthur Miller modeled on him for *A View from the Bridge*. We spent some wonderful hours among his memories of one friend's dangerous feud with "Tough Tony" Anastasio or another whose longshore activism had dropped off after "they broke his legs." This was the world I was after.

I'd first become interested in the waterfront when I lived in South Brooklyn, in a brownstone owned by an old Italian long-shoreman with missing fingers. Ships would occasionally appear at the end of my street, to be unloaded or repaired or sent off with a burst of nighttime fireworks. I grew familiar with the tug and ferry horns and watched the sunset flights of pigeons that zagged around the rooftops, much as in the famous Brando movie. But I knew almost nothing about the old days until I happened across a refer-ence to a 1940s newspaper series on waterfront gangsterism. It had run for twenty-four days—an extraordinary amount of space to give to any subject then, let alone to the lowly docks—and caused a national scandal; could the piers really have been as brutal as they looked in the movies?

When I met Jim Longhi again it was in his law offices on lower Broadway and he was wearing a beautiful brown suit. The high windows looked across to the old *New York Sun* building and be-yond to another waterfront, busy with beautifications. On a distant pier by the Brooklyn Bridge, where Longhi remembered watching desperate men fight a hook-swinging riot, a new riverside play-ground was being dug. We sat for an hour talking about some valiant old causes and vivid, long-dead thugs of the harbor.

Months before he died, I called Mr. Longhi once more at his office with a foolishly cinematic idea: to take my ninety-year-old friend out on a boat and tour the harbor, perhaps starting at the Narrows and hugging the shoreline to see what he remembered, pier by vestigial pier; Longhi would narrate as he drifted around the city, recalling who had owned what or done what to whom. ("You say, 'Mafia,' and it's provincial," he had told me. "You say, 'Mob,' and it extends way beyond the Italian underworld.")

The small tour boat *Geraldina* was ready to pick us up, her captain, herself a historian of the harbor, eagerly standing by with a video camera and microphone to capture the floating lecture. I then called Mr. Longhi to ease any remaining old-guy concerns about the trip, describing the level, relatively uncomplicated Chelsea dock (with an outdoor bar) where we imagined him stepping aboard after a steadying cocktail. He listened to my pitch, then paused and sighed into the phone. "It kind of sounds like a pain in the ass," he said at last. "I have my own picture of where everything was in my mind. I don't need to see the waterfront today to tell me that."

Seeing it today would indeed muddle things. At the edge of the Erie Basin, a ferry service lures visitors from Manhattan to a giant IKEA store that sits among the relics of the Brooklyn industrial waterfront. The store has a large upstairs cafeteria where, after a long afternoon touring housewares and furniture kits, you can eat Swedish meatballs and watch the sun lengthen across the car park, paved over a deep old dry dock that once held warships.

For decades, much of the abandoned waterfront was walled off by empty pier sheds. There was a forlorn beauty to the slow dilapidation, even if the water was blocked by a kind of ghost town. Many old sheds have since been flattened into parks; a trapeze school now sits atop Chelsea's Pier 40 building, and swinging out over the Hudson River waterfront, you have a clear downtown view uncluttered by slings or crates or Hi-Lo trucks. Looking out from the promenade that overhangs the expressway in Brooklyn Heights, you see a rotting wet railroad pier, all that remains here from Jim Longhi's time, the dark planking and rail track punctuated by shrubs that grow in green tufts; large concrete piers, recently cleared of their cargo sheds for park space, surround the ruin, which has been retained among the planned ice rink, new ballfields, and condominia pushing south from the bridges and toward the hugely still gantry cranes of the Red Hook Marine Terminal. Beyond the cranes sits the boxy white-brick headquarters of the Waterfront Commission of New York Harbor, established in the fifties to mind the gangsters on the docks and recently folded into Homeland Security.

The harbor Mr. Longhi kept in his head was the world's greatest port, a collection of bays rimmed with more than nine hundred piers and noisily crowded with hundreds of express liners, freighters, ferries, lighters, garbage scows, car floats, battleships, yachts, floating elevators, coffee barges, and constantly whistling tugs. The Hudson was still known as the North River (to distinguish it from the Delaware, or South River) along its length from the Battery, where freighters often lined up for their tug escorts, to the deep Midtown piers. This book is about that old waterfront, and its "criminal coloration," where money washed in and out, and graft mingled the longshore union with the racketeers.

Touring the harbor today, it is hard to imagine these quiet frontages of rot and renewal ever knowing such a fearful time that a reporter could write, "It has been said, and with some justification that the waterfront of New York produces more murders to the square foot than does any other one section of the country. Most such murders go unsolved." In fact, in 1948, the year the shooting of a young boss stevedore brought reporter Malcolm "Mike" Johnson of the *New York Sun* to the West Side docks, the Manhattan district attorney claimed there'd been at least two dozen unsolved waterfront murders since 1919. Johnson soon learned that snaking around the watery edges of his town was a very different city. "Murder on the waterfront is commonplace," he wrote, "a logical product of widespread gangsterism."

I have tried my best to evoke the dock world the longshoremen knew long before the newspapers discovered it. But at its heart, this is a reporter's story. If Mike Johnson's sleuthing along the docks has a hardboiled familiarity, echoing any number of later Mob tales involving hoods and rackets and an intrepid investigator, it is because his was the original—creating the Mob investigation form that runs from *On the Waterfront* to *The Valachi Papers* and *Donnie Brasco*. Johnson's discovery of what he called a "waterfront jungle" is also the story of a clash of New York institutions—a fading newspaper, backing its unshakable veteran star reporter; the Mob, near the height of its influence, whose leaders had largely come to power and of age during Prohibition; and the longshore union and the pugnacious survivor at its helm, "president-for-life" Joseph Ryan.

"One of the constantly astounding things about New York is that it can endure so much crime and corruption and still manage to get on," the *New York Herald Tribune* editorialized during the waterfront scandals. Indeed, the city had "gotten on" for several decades under an imaginary bargain, despite the occasional alarms raised by citizens' groups about port corruption and the bodies that turned up from month to month, deposited by what newspapers obtusely called the "dock wars." New Yorkers were aware that gangsters shared their town, primarily robbing and shooting one another and running the better nightclubs but never holding the reins completely as they had in Chicago. For many, their city's sinful reputation was the price of cosmopolitanism.

Reporters had toured the waterfront before Mike Johnson, dabbling in its rough atmosphere and lore as the movies did—as a setting for brawls and deals or other seamy behavior beyond the edge of society. Investigating the deaths of some twenty-one steve-dores in Brooklyn's Irishtown neighborhood, *The New Yorker*'s Alva Johnston wrote in 1931 that the total lack of arrests was "not because there is anything secret or underhand about these mur-ders, but because the witnesses won't talk." Loyalty to the water-front code against "squealing" also marked the death of the Brooklyn dock boss Red Donnelly, who, balehooked and shot in a waterfront shanty, was asked the perfunctory policeman's question of who had killed him. "John Doe," Red coughed out, and died pure.

Even the celebrated crimefighter Thomas Dewey, whose racket-busting exploits as Manhattan DA inspired a long-running radio drama (*Mister District Attorney*), was beaten by the docks and its infuriating code. After his agents secretly filmed longshoremen passing "tribute" money at two Wall Street piers in 1941, they sub-poenaed two hundred of the men and shuttled them in buses to a special screening of the surveillance movie, which failed to con-vince many about testifying. As one asked, "Who the hell wants to be a dead hero, mister?"

Arturo Piecoro began his three decades on the New York docks in the last days of the "shape-up" system, when each freight-bearing vessel that entered the harbor was met by gangs of men, many carrying curved iron hooks with which they would dig out the stowed cargoes of lumber, coffee, copper ingots, or Egyptian cotton. These hopefuls crowded together at the pierheads, hunching under their caps and windbreakers in raw weather, waiting to be chosen in an ancient ritual in which most would be sent home. The shape-up was "a hit-and-miss thing unless you knew somebody," Piecoro told me at a Brooklyn coffee shop. "If you miss one shape, you hurry down to the next pier. There's another ship. You bullshit with some guys, then go over. Three steady gangs would be called first; then, if somebody was sick, you might have a chance."

Those picked in the shape might work four or sixteen hours while a particular ship remained in port; if they weren't part of a regular work gang, they could idle for a week around the piers or waterfront bars, scanning the newspapers or pub chalkboards for lists of incoming ships. When they worked, the longies, as they called themselves, were at greatest risk down in the ship's hold; but up top, slings could slip and rain down heavy cargo loads on the men working below. On Columbia Street in Brooklyn, the day's gangs were often sorted out between the hatch boss and hiring boss before the shape-up whistle even sounded, which made the shape-up itself a demoralizing formality. "Guys paid for jobs, but you never saw it," Piecoro told me. "They might turn up with something on their hat, or behind their ear, but you never saw them do it. That was all done before."

When Jim Longhi brought his friend Arthur Miller down to Columbia Street to show him a shape-up, the young playwright was thoroughly shocked to see the men herded docilely together, "waiting for the hiring boss, on whose arrival they surged forward and formed in a semicircle to attract his pointing finger and the numbered brass checks that guaranteed a job for the day," Miller remembered. On another visit he saw men "tearing at each other's hands" in "a frantic scramble" for the morning's last few work checks. "America, I thought, stopped at Columbia Street."

So it seemed. "Mobsters and labor racketeers" controlled the world's largest port, Mike Johnson wrote in 1948—and they threatened his life for saying it. The bolder pier heists included an entire electrical generator gone missing and a vanished ten-ton shipment of steel. Organized pilferage was so rampant, Johnson said, it amounted to an unofficial national tax, made possible by wider corruption in the longshore union and in the courts, the police department, and Washington. The scandal he raised inspired Estes Kefauver to put mobsters on national television and the filmmakers

Budd Schulberg and Elia Kazan to create a controversial master-piece. That so many people now regard *On the Waterfront* as an allegory for something else—the filmmakers' own testifying to Congress about communism—shows how much has been forgotten about the criminal reality of the docks Mike Johnson exposed.

As Johnson would learn, the "waterfront jungle" was by no means a clear extension of the New York it encircled. It was a city apart, with its own bosses, language, and codes, bankers, soldiers and even martyrs, a frontier all its own.

DARK HARBOR

CHAPTER 1

"DOV'È PANTO?"

The pier where Pietro Panto worked jutted into the brackish current of the East River just upstream from the cabled span of the Brooklyn Bridge, looking across to the ferry sheds and the bottom of Manhattan. At five o'clock in the afternoon of Friday, July 14, 1939, Pete Panto left the Moore-McCormack pier, where he served as hiring foreman, and headed home to his rooming house near the Brooklyn Navy Yard. An affable, dark-eyed young man in work clothes and a fedora, he was wiry but strong, a black mustache above an easy smile that sometimes showed a gap in his teeth. In his room on North Elliott Place he was shaving for a date later that evening with his fiancée, Alice Maffia, when her younger brother, Michael, came to the room with word that Panto had a telephone call at the corner cigar store. Panto wiped his face and made his way downstairs, but when he returned from his conversation his mood had darkened. He seemed uncharacteristically spooked as he told Michael he would be meeting "two tough mugs" or "men I don't like" for an hour or so that night, warning, "If I don't get back by ten o'clock tomorrow morning, tell the police."

Panto left behind his wallet and an empty suitcase; his work clothes were still laid out on his bed when a car appeared out front around seven. He was dressed in his best suit and a dark hat for his later outing with Alice when he climbed inside and saw two men he knew from the longshoremen's union, Emil Camarda and Gus Scannavino, riding with someone less familiar. He took his seat with the others; then the sedan rolled away down North Elliott Place and into the summer evening, and Pete Panto was gone.

Panto had arrived on the Brooklyn waterfront sometime in the mid-thirties, a young longshoreman whose accent hinted he had divided his life between Brooklyn and southern Italy. Brooklyn was then home to dry docks and repair basins as well as warehousing and shipping terminals and the great Navy Yard. After a period of breaking-in along the docks, Panto got his union card in 1937, and at age twenty-six he secured a regular job at the Moore-McCormack line's Pier 15, at the foot of Brooklyn Heights.

The five-mile stretch of Brooklyn shore that ran south from the Brooklyn Bridge to Twentieth Street was overwhelmingly staffed by Italians like him, many of them recent immigrants who worked the less desirable cargoes. The six Italian "locals" of the International Longshoremen's Association were overseen by Vice-President Emil Camarda, a waterfront patriarch with a foot in the legitimate world and whose family used their union titles to act as middlemen in many of the docks' predatory side businesses. Some fourteen thousand dockers labored in "Camarda locals" such as Panto's, many of them in the area called Red Hook, which stretched between the Buttermilk Channel and the Gowanus Canal. The Camardas' home rule had the distant blessing of the union's quotable longtime president Joe Ryan, whose organization in Manhattan had been dominated since the teens by the West Side Irish. "Over in Brooklyn" was a favorite phrase of Ryan's to express his bewilderment with events across the East River, a shoreline he saw dense with alien Italians and Red insurgents kept in rough order by the Camarda clan.

As if his union weren't already welcoming enough to gangsters, Emil Camarda helped found Brooklyn's City Democratic Club, quartered in a Clinton Street building owned by a Mafia leader named Vincent Mangano. Inside, longshore union figures could do business with local mobsters under friendly cover of pinochle games. Mangano was committee chairman for the club's annual Columbus Day Ball, held at the Hotel St. George in Brooklyn Heights, whose program boasted pages bought by other syndicate men: Joe Profaci, Albert Anastasia, and Joe Adonis. Pete Panto soon discovered the direct connection between the political club and the waterfront rackets: longshoremen bought thousands of tickets to the ball as a suggested "donation" toward getting dock work; "eight or ten thousand" sold for a ballroom that held only "four or five hundred people," he told his friend the Brooklyn labor lawyer Marcy Protter. Often, the ticket money was already deducted from their pay envelopes. (A Brownsville mobster arrested for murder in 1939 was carrying several hundred unsold tickets, with the sellers' names—Hugo, Foxie, Battling Joe, Sharky—scribbled on the back.)

Beyond the ordinary pier crap games and policy lotteries that drained longshoremen's pay, Panto encountered other kickbacks and tributes: "In order to obtain work on a certain pier," he explained to Protter, "you had to enter into a form of contract to have all your haircuts at a certain barbershop, and you paid in advance, each month, for those haircuts." Likewise, every fall, many longshoremen were obliged to buy their wine grapes from a designated dealer at lush prices, whether they planned to make wine or not. Panto claimed that many longshoremen paid out almost half their wages in kickbacks to qualify for work, and that union meetings in the Camarda locals were almost never held. Dockers did whatever was needed to gain favor in the shape, including buying into the pier boss's "hiring clubs," taking loans from waterfront loan sharks, and accepting gang-cutting (fifteen men doing the work of a full gang of twenty, with the "ghost" pay going to the hiring boss), which compounded the risks in an industry where mangling injuries were common but insurance scarce. Longshoring ranked near tree topping among deadly occupations.

A man who can inspire loyalty in his crew is always useful, and Panto rose to hiring boss by 1939, despite his feelings about the racketeers. But he was soon rousing unity beyond his own pier, joining his local's Rank and File Committee of men attracted by the gains won on the West Coast docks by the radical Harry Bridges. "Pete Panto was a very dynamic person, and he was a good speaker in Italian, and he held a number of public meetings," Sam Madell, a longtime Communist organizer of Brooklyn longshoremen, later told an interviewer. "We are strong," Panto reminded his men, "all we have to do is stand up and fight."

In the spring of 1939, Panto led a series of increasingly large and rowdy meetings. Crowding before the piers at night, hundreds of men applauded his speeches demanding union democracy— regular shop meetings and an end to the shape-up and kickback system. In mid-June, 350 union men heard him speak about waterfront corruption, and he addressed a still-larger group on July 3. What the rank and file viewed as a reform movement, however, the Camardas and Joe Ryan saw simply as an insurgency, and union spokesmen vilified Panto as a dangerous Red even as Rank and File leafletters were roughed up along the docks. In early July, the casual threats Panto had heard around Columbia Street in Red Hook and dismissed with a grin escalated to a formal summons. Emil Camarda called him to his waterfront office.

When Panto arrived at the dock end of President Street, he noticed Camarda was accompanied by several hired men, "some of whom he knew by reputation," Marcy Protter reported. Panto refused to speak in front of these "henchmen," and Camarda sent them from the room, leaving the patriarch of the Brooklyn waterfront alone with the young leader of the dock rebels: "[I]n the course of the conversation," Protter explained, Camarda told Panto that "he personally liked Pete, and thought he was a very fine fellow, but some of the boys didn't like some of the things he was doing and saying, and he advised him that maybe it would be better if he stopped what he was doing."

Panto refused. Camarda's warning about "some of the boys" was deadly Red Hook code for the Mob's displeasure. Friends from the Rank and File Committee cautioned Panto that his life was now in danger, that he should never travel alone. Panto repeated that he would not be intimidated, but agreed to be more cautious about traveling unguarded. At his last meeting, days before his disappearance, he surrounded himself with some 1,250 longshoremen in South Brooklyn's Star Hall, which echoed with the rough eloquence of his Italian speechmaking and the catcalls of the men. But mixed clumsily into the crowd were observers sent by Albert Anastasia.

That summer, the World's Fair brought thousands to Queens to see the Trylon and Perisphere, the Belgium Pavilion Tower and World of Tomorrow. But it became a fearful season along the Brooklyn waterfront, where a graffiti campaign began with the dockworkers whose revolt Peter Panto had been leading when he vanished on July 14. It began within days, *Dov'è Panto?* ("Where is Panto?") scrawled in anger along the Red Hook piers, on freight cars, trucks, and warehouses, marking walls in the Italian longshoring neighborhoods, puzzling outsiders like a foreign code when it reached the blue-slate walks above the harbor. The plea spread from the water's edge to subway walls and the sides of downtown Brooklyn office buildings, and leaflets titled "Where Is Pete Panto?" littered the area near the Navy Yard.

Each sodden corpse that bumped to the surface of the rivers around New York was hauled out and checked against photographs of the smiling young hero of the docks. Panto's friends worried in the press that his body had been irrecoverably "weighted down with stones" on the harbor floor or swept along with the night tides that ran from Sandy Hook to Hell Gate. "Coppers are worried about Pete Panto, a courageous dockworker, who was bothering Brooklyn banditi," the gossip columnist Walter Winchell announced. "Police fear Pete is wearing a cement suit at the bottom of the East River." When the Communist *Daily Worker* put its writer on the mystery, he discovered that Panto had been immediately replaced by a more obedient hiring boss and that Italian longshoremen refused to speak for print except anonymously. "We are men with families," one explained, "and want to live."

Years before he inherited a jumble of unsolved killings on his office wall in 1939, the new Brooklyn district attorney, William O'Dwyer, had walked the dock beat as a Brooklyn patrolman during the early rum-running days of Prohibition. By the end of his eight years as a cop, he'd seen the "sporadic gangsterism" of the Kid Cheese gang and the Kilduff brothers give way to what he called the "gay lark," when "the criminal was made respectable" under the Volstead Act. Bill O'Dwyer's approach to his adopted city was tempered by his having been both a cop and, before that, a seminarian. The waterfront was about as far as an Irish immigrant could get from the cloistered life O'Dwyer had tried and abandoned before arriving in New York in 1910. A husky, dark-browed man whose soft brogue came and went as needed, "Bill-O" favored "a good meal and a good chin" with friends, and his circle steadily grew. The fact that he'd become Brooklyn DA in less than twenty years was in part a credit to the expansive force of his personality.

The clammy stone prison in Lower Manhattan popularly called the Tombs was connected to the Criminal Courts building by an iron walkway, along which families huddled below might catch a glimpse of their prisoner loved ones; this catwalk in turn had its own nickname, the Bridge of Sighs, after the gloomy limestone passageway in Venice. And far uptown from the Tombs, the Bronx County Jail was known to many inside as "the DA's singing school." In January 1940, one of Bill O'Dwyer's old friends from his patrolman days, John Osnato, was in a Bronx jail cell talking in falsely sympathetic tones to a Brooklyn hoodlum named Dukey Maffetore, who was known mainly for chauffeuring mysterious trunkloads for his bosses in a Brownsville, Brooklyn, mob. Maffetore had been named by another prisoner in the execution of one recently murdered criminal, Red Alpert. Lieutenant Osnato spoke to Maffetore in the intimate Italian dialect of his household, something seldom heard from city cops. In an era when interrogation subjects were commonly beaten and thrown around, Lieutenant Osnato was an early master of a subtler technique now called good cop/bad cop. "I don't know how much longer I can keep them outside," he'd announce to his panicked subject as fellow detectives pounded the door.

Osnato was already respected among the city's cops for having arrested young Al Capone in 1925 after a Christmas night shooting of Irish gangsters in Red Hook near the Gowanus Canal. (Seeing Capone and a friend come into the Adonis Social Club with two blond dates, the Irishtown dock leader Pegleg Lonergan had fatally remarked, "What the hell are them white girls doing with a pair of greaseballs?"); and in 1934, after gunmen brought off the largest American cash heist to date, $427,000, from a Rubel Ice Company truck, Osnato headed the enormous manhunt.

Osnato turned criminals into informers as naturally as Bill O'Dwyer made friends. In the case of Dukey Maffetore, the obedient chauffeur of dead "packages" for a Brownsville gang, Osnato and his partner were masterful in breaking him down with false kindness, playing on the hoodlum's love of family and sugaring visits to his Bronx jail cell with packs of Pall Mall cigarettes. The lieutenant brought news from the outside that Maffetore's superiors were living lushly, letting him take the blame for the murder of Red Alpert. When Maffetore finally weakened, Osnato appeared one afternoon in O'Dwyer's office to make the quiet announcement: " 'The Duke' will talk to you."

Maffetore named a member of the gang's low-level "troops," "Pretty" Levine, who also began unburdening himself. This news pricked the confidence of his criminal superior, Abe Reles, a five-foot-two-inch killer and Brownsville gang leader whom O'Dwyer's office had sitting in Manhattan's Tombs for the same Red Alpert killing. As he waited in his cell, separated from his colleagues but surrounded by appalling rumors of their confessions, Reles began to consider the unthinkable option himself. He would need no prompting in person, since O'Dwyer's detectives had already created the climate of snitching. On the eve of Good Friday 1940, Reles sent a note to his wife, "Go and see O'Dwyer and tell him I want to talk to him."

At the time, Reles was a thirty-four-year-old leader in the Brooklyn underworld, and the likely whereabouts of Peter Panto was only part of a bloody catalogue of things he claimed to know. He had risen from petty hoodlum, crippler of shopkeepers late on their protection payments, and killer of car washers who tried his patience to become a senior figure in the syndicate execution ring overseen by Albert Anastasia. Cruel and boastful, with a character that one reporter called "queasy," Reles was also known as Kid Twist, a street moniker imaginatively attributed to his strong, thick-fingered hands and strangling prowess, but originally a thug homage to a boyhood gang hero on the Lower East Side. "This fellow is brave enough to stab in the back, or shoot a defenseless person, and, with a gang supporting him, might punch or kick an invalid or a near invalid," declared one Kings County judge, but he would "never stand up to a square man-to-man fight."

Reles was smuggled out of the Tombs under guard in the middle of the night, passing through the high, fat pillars of Brooklyn's Municipal Building at three in the morning and bluntly telling detectives when he reached the fourth floor that he was hungry. "We were cautious lest this announcement be part of a jailbreak plan," O'Dwyer later wrote of their predawn meeting in his office. "I sent out for a sandwich and coffee and watched him as he ate." While O'Dwyer thought he had scored the cooperation of a formidable Brooklyn gangster, the man eating the sandwich was a much bigger catch than that, poised to betray an organization (called the Combination by members) whose full national reach was still not suspected by most law enforcement. Before Reles began speaking, "I had no notion . . . that there was organized crime all over the country," O'Dwyer later admitted. "I didn't know any more than anyone else knew." Reles warned him of the Combination's power, conceding he was probably a marked man whether he testified or not. "There ain't a man in the world they can't get if they go after him."

O'Dwyer locked Reles in a comfortable suite at the nearby Bossert Hotel, once known for its rooftop dancing. In his rooms, over twelve days of breathtaking confession, the Kid unspooled an epic gangster narrative in such commanding detail that by the end, his ghoulish dictation had filled twenty-five notebooks with remembered pluggings, ice-pickings, stranglings, and incinerations. "By the eleventh day he was going at such a rate that investigation of extortions he exposed had to be set aside in order to keep up with his listing of homicides," Assistant DA Burton Turkus wrote. In several cases, while accounting for at least sixty-three New York murders, Reles explained killings the authorities had never heard of. No one at his level had ever confessed to murder, let alone to scores of them. All he asked was complete immunity.

"In Brooklyn," Reles told the DA, "we are all together with the mob on the docks." While the connection of the longshore union with waterfront racketeering was long established, Burton Turkus noted that no one before had ever shown its role in something as large as the Combination. With Reles's corroboration of dozens of killings, O'Dwyer announced he had a "perfect" case against Albert Anastasia. This drew several visits to the DA's office by Emil Camarda, attempting to slow the pace of the investigation. But O'Dwyer never had Anastasia brought in for questioning in the Panto disappearance or any other murder.

Anastasia's homicidal reputation terrified gangsters, dockworkers, and potential witnesses alike. In photographs, he is usually caught on the way to a court or a crime committee appearance, his face that of a plump, dark-headed bully boy smirking on his way to the principal's. The young Umberto Anastasio, one of nine sons of an Italian longshoreman, arrived from Calabria as a barefoot shipjumper not far from the Brooklyn waterfront he would ultimately control. Working on the New York piers, Anastasia killed his first longshoreman as a teenager in 1917, and rose within the flourishing criminal gangs of the Prohibition years when the Italians successfully battled the Irish for control of the Brooklyn docks. In 1931, he was one of four gunmen who murdered "Joe the Boss" Masseria in a Coney Island restaurant on behalf of Joe's lunch partner, Lucky Luciano, who had stepped away to take "a long leak."

By the mid-1930s Anastasia managed the execution arm of the Combination under the industrial racketeer Louis "Lepke" Buchalter. No Combination murder occurred without Anastasia's approval if not also his fervent planning. His systematic squad of largely

Jewish and Italian murderers served the recently organized national syndicate and invented the anonymous "contract" killing. When the full gruesome picture of the syndicate's killing "troop" emerged, the press (led by the *World-Telegram*'s Harry Feeney) called the organization Murder Inc., with Anastasia the outfit's "Lord High Executioner," a tabloid honor that can't have entirely displeased him.

Reles helped build successful cases against other Murder Inc. figures, including Anastasia's partner Louis "Lepke"—who'd been hidden in Brooklyn stash houses by Anastasia for two years despite a national FBI manhunt and a $25,000 bounty—and Lepke's assistant in the rackets, Emanuel (Mendy) Weiss. Along the way, Reles told what he'd heard about the fate of a labor organizer who'd been threatening the Combination's holdings on the Brooklyn docks.

In December 1940, O'Dwyer hired a steam shovel team to begin digging in the frozen marsh along the eastern bank of the Passaic River, near the Lyndhurst, New Jersey, house of an Anastasia man named Jimmy Ferraco. Reles described the Ferraco chicken farm as a favorite dumping ground for the bodies of Mob victims. The hard winter dig brought up nothing for two weeks. Then, after consulting again with Reles and lesser informers, O'Dwyer refined the exact location of the grave and the steam shovels resumed scratching at the frozen earth. In late January 1941, eighteen months after Peter Panto's abduction, a canvas sack emerged containing a decomposing body trussed up in rope. One of the diggers was Panto's friend from the docker revolt, Pete Mazzie, a stocky twenty-three-year-old longshoreman who, as he knelt at the grave scrutinizing the emerging lump of body, rock, and earth, resembled a streetwise hero John Garfield might have played. The corpse was coated in quicklime, a Combination method for rendering victims unrecognizable, but Mazzie firmly identified his friend's remains from a familiar gap in his teeth. Then the whole frozen mound was dug out and brought on an open truck under police escort (for fear the Mob would hijack the corpse) back to the Brooklyn morgue.

Reles's information had again proved roughly true. But on the day after the morgue identification, on February 7, 1941, a tall, thin lower-placed defector from Murder Inc., Allie "Tick Tock" Tannenbaum, made his own visit to the Brooklyn Municipal Building and offered a more precise solution to the Panto mystery: One day in late July 1939, Tannenbaum had pulled his car into the parking spaces near the lake in Prospect Park in Brooklyn. For several minutes he sat and waited on a nearby bench until the car of Mendy Weiss drew up. Weiss, a dark-eyed, thickly built man of well over two hundred pounds, joined him on the bench, where they could hear the sounds of summer boaters on the water. Then the two began to walk together, exchanging informational pleasantries about their ugly business until Tannenbaum spotted vicious scratches all over Weiss's broad hands. " 'What happened to you?' " he asked. " 'What did you do, fight with some girl?' "

" 'We had a close one the other night,' " Tannenbaum remembered Weiss explaining. "I said, 'Yeah.' So he goes on to tell me that [Jimmy] Ferraco, Anastasio, and himself were in a house waiting for somebody to bring some wop out there that they were supposed to kill and bury. He said, 'The guy just stepped into the door and must have realized what it was about and he tried to get out. He almost got out. . . . If I wasn't there he would have got away. I grabbed him and mugged him, and when I mugged him, he started to fight and he tried to break the mug and that's when he scratched me, but he didn't get away.' I said, 'What was it about?' He said, 'It's Panto, some guy Albert had a lot of trouble with down in the waterfront and he was threatening to get Albert into a lot of trouble.' "

Tannenbaum's low-key but extraordinary account of his walk in the park with Panto's killer was dutifully taken down by Assistant

DA Edward Heffernan of O'Dwyer's office. Then it was just as carefully laid deep in a file, where it sat for another thirteen years.

Buddy Scotto was just a boy when his father, Patsy, held the ceremony for "what was left of Peter Panto," leaving from the family's Brooklyn funeral home on April 19, 1941. Mobsters were an intimidating part of the local Brooklyn landscape, Buddy recalls. "We all knew who these people were. You said hello to them and that's that." But, despite being terrified, "My father had a sneaky amount of guts." As docker pallbearers bore the casket past the City Democratic Club, where the need for Panto's removal had so often been discussed by Mob men, Patsy Scotto walked at the head of the sad parade. Hundreds of longshoremen turned out that Saturday, hoping for a final look. "I remember the overwhelming response. The longshoremen really stepped out to make a statement." Many crowded outside Sacred Heart church during the Mass, holding commemorative copies of the docker newspaper *Shape-Up*, which honored the day with a poem:

> Drop hooks all you longshoremen
> This Panto burial day
> This working man from off the docks
> Our martyr in the fray

"Pete became a saint like they carry on St. Anthony's Day," remembered the waterfront veteran Jim Longhi decades later, looking from his Manhattan law office toward the Brooklyn shore. "Everybody knew who did the job on Pete." Everybody knew, and yet while Abe Reles helped the Brooklyn DA send seven senior members of Murder Inc. to the electric chair—including Louis Lepke, the highest-ranking mobster ever to be executed—the legal assault stopped short of touching Anastasia himself.

Weeks before the Lepke conviction, early on the morning of

November 20, 1941, Reles dove, fell, or was hurled from the sixth-floor window of his guarded seaside room at Coney Island's Half Moon Hotel, where the detail of six policemen were all asleep, or so they later claimed. Detectives were left to decode a crude rope twisted together out of hotel sheets and some wire and wrapped around the dead gangster dressed in dark clothes. Any case against Anastasia, O'Dwyer insisted in later years, went "out the window" with Kid Twist. Anastasia had eluded O'Dwyer's investigators for months, but he quickly reemerged with the death of Reles.

Weeks later there was partial justice for Panto when the verdicts came down on Murder Inc.'s Louis "Lepke" Buchalter and his assistants Louis Capone and Mendy Weiss, the man who confessed the fatal "mugging" of Panto to Allie Tannenbaum and had regretted the Panto job to Reles: "I hated to take that kid." The three men had been tried together for another of Weiss's dozens of Mob murders, that of a former garment trucker and witness against Lepke. At the trial's end, Lepke accepted the announcement of his death sentence with a fidgety silence. Before his own verdict, Mendy Weiss blared out, "All I can say is I'm innocent," then ranted at prosecutors, "You got my blood. How that Captain Bals can frame a guy."

The man he blamed, DA O'Dwyer's head investigator, Captain Frank Bals, had presided over security when the prosecution's star, Abe Reles, plunged from the Half Moon Hotel weeks earlier. With the Reles disaster still fresh, Bals eyed Weiss as the condemned man stalked past to exit the courtroom. Then, emboldened by the death verdict, Bals spat out a line he must have long been saving: "Peter Panto is waiting for you."

There it all stood when the war came, speeding up the work even as it drained the docks of draft-age men and filled the harbor with warships. After the war, with Bill O'Dwyer having left Brooklyn to become mayor of New York, many of the waterfront powers from the time of Panto's rebellion—the gangsters, dock bosses, politicians, even a rumored master of the port called "Mr. Big"—remained firmly in charge when a newspaperman with a similar crusading instinct made his way down to the water.

CHAPTER 2

STIRRING UP THE ANIMALS

The Sun Building stood huge and marble white just north of City Hall, tiered with large windows and seizing a full block on lower Broadway. At either corner on its avenue side hung big clocks housed in bronze—one declaring *Sun* time; the other, a round thermometer, showed the official temperature quoted regularly by copyboys craning from the city room window. The clocks had been a welcoming touch added by the paper's new owner, Frank A. Munsey, soon after he bought the site in 1916. Visitors from either direction—Broadway tourists, city politicians, or reporters arriving with hat brims low after a hard night at the Panama or the Reade Way bar—passed under the clocks with their cheerful engraved legend: "The Sun—It Shines for All."

Mike Johnson first entered beneath these clocks in the fall of 1928, arriving at work with the details for a story about a minor traffic accident he'd noticed on his way. A dark stairway climbed from the lobby to the second floor, where visitors to the newspaper met an old man with a shock of white hair who had been gatekeeping, the staff joked, since Lincoln was shot. Once you passed Mr. Chandler, the city room opened into what must have seemed a clattering paradise to a reporter fresh from Macon, Georgia. A newspaper rack held every rival New York paper laid out flat; then came a short horseshoe of desktops where pale men in white sleeves scrutinized copy to the clacking of typewriters, drilling of telephones, and occasional shouts of "Boy!"

Across the great room, oak desks were clustered in lamplit banks, while farther in, past the clippings morgue, was the buzzing Teletype room. Stuffed into a heavy leather tube called the chute, finished copy left the city room's central island of editors' desks and was shuttled along an air-compressor system, like a cashier's sending for a price at Wanamaker's, back to the starkly lit composing room to be set. All of this nervous work finally fed down to the building's huge presses in the basement, where the trucks heavy with fresh editions pulled out from the *Sun*'s Reade Street side, then rolled down Broadway toward the bridges and Brooklyn or turned north to drop bundles of market finals thumping all over Midtown for the train commuters home.

"I got a story on my way here," Mike Johnson cockily announced that first day when he met the night editor, Walter Whitman, "a hatchet-faced little man with gray hair, gray mustache, and a Texas drawl." "That's fine," Whitman jadedly answered and handed the new man a sheaf of other stories about minor motor accidents from the past twelve hours. "You can include your story with these."

By the forties, Johnson had reported everything for the *Sun* from the burning of the steamship *Morro Castle* and the Lindbergh kidnapping trial, to cataclysms in Europe and Asia, to the attack on Cassino and the aftermath of an atomic bomb, and had become the paper's general assignment star. He stood five foot seven and was a strongly packed 165 pounds, with a wide, intelligent face, black hair swept back, and dark-circled eyes. Though he was known around the floor for his self-mocking humor, in his more official portraits there was something sad in the eyes. The great sportswriter W. C. Heinz, who started out as a *Sun* copyboy, remembered a stocky, broad-shouldered man who could be broodily focused while engrossed in a story, lucidly funny when released from it. Heinz recalled meeting Johnson while still a copyboy, when "he was not one of my favorite characters, under the surface a little morose maybe."

The *Sun* had begun life sensationally in 1833, as the city's first successful penny newspaper, reaching ten thousand readers after only a year, and then gained further strength in 1835 through a brilliant fraud—an extraordinary series of articles chronicling the lunar discoveries of the English astronomer Sir John Herschel and his giant telescope: rich jungles, volcanoes, miniature lunar bison; a tailless, upright-walking beaver that "carries its young in its arms" and knew the secrets of fire; and, the denouement, villages full of real live "Man-bats." No one was more astonished by Herschel's discoveries than the astronomer himself.

The *Sun*'s journalistic prime arrived just after the Civil War, when the editor Charles A. Dana helped introduce what became known as "personal" reporting, and Dana's city editor, John Bogart, coined the lasting definition: "When a dog bites a man, that is not news, because it happens so often. But if a man bites a dog, that is news." Dana died in 1897, the year his paper published the most reprinted article in its history, Francis P. Church's response to the query of a young New York City girl about Santa Claus. "The only Christmas gift I ever got from the *Sun*," Mike Johnson groused to a later employer on receiving his first bonus, "was a fancy re-print of that God-damn editorial, 'Yes, Virginia, There is a Santa Claus.' The publisher sent it out one year to all the employees, infuriating everybody."

The staid, masculine world of the *Sun* was housed in what was once America's first department store, A. T. Stewart Dry Goods, a five-floor retail building nicknamed the "marble palace." After Frank Munsey fitted the old marble palace with clocks to announce his newspaper, the upstairs windows burned all night with the work of the newsroom's night shift. Munsey added a separate room for smoking and congregating, an innovation that left the *Sun*'s city room less cloudy than others but gave reporters a hiding place if they wanted to put off their next assignment. Some old *Sun* hands on the night shift worked smokelessly at their desks, chewing dead cigars beneath their eyeshades.

The *Sun* was a comparatively reserved workplace even when going full panic on a big fire. Visitors from more raucous newsrooms likened it to a museum. "It was really quiet," remembered Bill Heinz. "There was no shouting in the newsroom and no smoking, of course. If a big story came in, there was a brief noise until someone was assigned to it." One day during World War II, when Mr. Chandler somehow wasn't watching the door, "a Western Union girl with a Mailgram rollerskated into the city room shouting, 'Does anyone know a Keats Speed?'" recalled Joan O'Sullivan, who started as a wartime copygirl. "It was like a bomb went off." During Mike Johnson's time there, the newsroom's tone was an echo from the Frank Munsey era, embodied by the remote and soft-spoken man sitting in the northeast corner, the paper's distinguished executive editor, Keats Speed.

Known even to his oldest staff only as Mr. Speed (or, privately, "the man in the corner"), he was a Kentuckian and great-nephew, on his mother's side, of the English poet John Keats. Speed had been an aristocratic fixture in his shop since coming over to the *Sun* in the twenties, and by the forties still wore his white hair slicked and center-parted in the Mencken style. Next to winning a

Pulitzer, gaining the approval of Mr. Speed was the highest accomplishment for a *Sun* writer.

Johnson would remember him as "unfailingly courteous but strictly formal, maintaining a polite reserve that few could penetrate." Speed was born on a sixty-acre horse farm, had for several years attended a girls' school with his four older sisters, and then, as a young man, was offered a position playing for Louisville's pro baseball team. This he turned down under family pressure, only to enter the slightly more reputable field of journalism. In Speed's own judgment, he had made "a lousy reporter." But as an editor, he proved an able manager and nimble survivor through the collapse and reorganization of several newspapers, arriving at the *Sun* after his *New York Press* was bought and sacrificed to it by Mr. Munsey, called "the newspaper butcher" or "the great amalgamator" for his habit of buying and folding competing papers, what he called "killing and creating to find the public's taste." (By the time of Munsey's death in 1925, he had winnowed the New York newspaper field from seven morning dailies to four and from seven afternoon dailies to five, while fattening his *Sun* along the way.)

The *Sun*'s city editor, Edmond Bartnett, whom Mike Johnson called "the best boss I ever had," could be gracious and detached like the patrician Keats Speed, but a poker face masked his "softhearted" nature. Bart, as he was called by a privileged set around the newsroom, sat near Speed along the eastern wall. He had originally considered the priesthood before drifting into news. "Bartnett was a very gentle man, and it was sort of surprising to find such a gentle man in that job," recalled Bill Heinz. Bart "assumed a rather austere manner that fooled no one," Mike Johnson wrote, and the staff loved him despite the complaint that "he nurses a drink until it boils." (Two *Sun* writers once drank so late in a basement booth at a nearby saloon that they were forgotten and locked downstairs for the night; they climbed out through a coal chute, only to emerge in the middle of Chambers Street "just as Edmond Bartnett was walking along to work," said Joan O'Sullivan. "They just fell in step with him, hungover and covered in coal dust, and went to work.")

It was Bart who dispatched Johnson to cover the Lindbergh kidnapping trial and the burning of the *Morro Castle*; Bart who trusted his general assignment man to serve as the paper's Broadway columnist just before the war, then made him war correspondent in the Pacific theater, where Johnson covered fleet operations and the Okinawa invasion, the desolation of Hiroshima and the Japanese surrender. (Bart would talk each day to the anxious wives of his war reporters.)

During the war's closing days, when Bill Heinz was covering the European theater and Johnson was in the South Pacific, another *Sun* copyboy who later made good as a sportswriter, Dave Anderson, was following both men's dispatches almost as closely as he did each afternoon's box scores. In between the stifling subway rides to pick up ad copy from Gimbels or Best or Macy's, Anderson recalled that there were the privileged times, too: when "you could go downstairs and get the papers fresh off the press," hold the ink-damp A-bomb and VJ Day editions, with Johnson's cabled stories, as they rolled out.

Malcolm Malone Johnson was born in the Blue Ridge Mountain town of Clermont, Georgia, in 1904, and grew up close by, in Gainesville. Johnson's father, a lawyer, expected his eldest of six children to follow him into the profession. His mother, Willie Estelle Johnson, was an equally strong figure who had been a schoolteacher before marriage. As reconstructed by Mike's son, the journalist and historian Haynes Johnson, for a collection of his father's reporting, William Johnson "was a scholarly man, and a deacon of his church, but he was somewhat reserved and distant. Mike worshipped him but never felt like he really knew him."

From the father, Mike inherited determination, especially in the face of thuggery, as William Johnson had shown in denouncing the Ku Klux Klan during the notorious case of Leo Frank. Among the things Mike Johnson most admired later about his father was his brave involvement in the defense of Frank, the Jewish pencil factory manager accused of raping and killing a thirteen-year-old girl, Mary Phagan, in Atlanta. Frank was ultimately lynched in 1914. The case divided people across the country, and drove recruitment in the Klan's subsequent revival in Georgia. "My father apparently had a very good reputation for briefing a case," Malcolm Johnson told his son Haynes in a taped interview, "and he'd been called in to help brief for the defense. . . . He thought Frank was innocent and he was framed." William Johnson died in the Great Influenza Epidemic of 1918, when Mike was thirteen. By taking in boarders, his widowed mother was somehow able to get all six of her children to college.

Released from the law track his father had urged on him, the young Johnson got his first glimpse of a new career through running the high school paper. At Mercer College, a journalism class lured him into work at the Macon *Telegraph*, a center of learning that ultimately replaced his formal education. Among the books he studied while still at school was Frank O'Brien's *The Story of the Sun*, in which one of the paper's longtime editors, Edward P. Mitchell, nobly quoted his old boss, Charles A. Dana:

> Mr. Dana wrote more than half a century ago to one of his associates, "Your articles have stirred up the animals, which you as well as I recognize as one of the great ends of life." Sometimes he used Titania's wand; sometimes he used a red hot poker. Not only in that great editor's time but in that of his predecessors and successors the *Sun* has held it to be a duty and a joy to assist to the best

of its ability in the discouragement of anything like lethargy in the menagerie.

By the time he went north, Mike Johnson had already learned the importance of stirring up the animals, having endangered his life reporting on the Klan. "I came to New York from Georgia, my native state, after working three years as a reporter on the Macon (Ga.) *Telegraph*," he later wrote.

I was fortunate in getting my initial training under the brilliant Mark F. Ethridge, then the *Telegraph*'s managing editor . . . On the recommendation of Ethridge, an alumnus of the *Sun*, the city editor Edmond P. Bartnett, hired me, sight unseen. This was most unusual, I was told, thereby increasing my nervousness. I had never been in New York before and I was thrilled, but also scared to death that I would not make good in Big City journalism.

In fact, when he reached New York his work had stormily preceded him. Johnson's series of investigative pieces about the Ku Klux Klan in Toombs County, Georgia, in the rural center of the state, documented Klan financial abuses as well as night rides and floggings of anti-Klan lawyers and newspaper editors. The *Telegraph* stories also ran on the front page of Joseph Pulitzer's New York *World*, then the most prestigious newspaper in America, and *The New York Times* editorialized on the Toombs County raids, its writer clearly educated by young Johnson's gutsy investigations. ("Hooded men," reported the *Times*, "whether members of the Klan or rascally pretenders, seem to be intimidating Toombs County.") A solicitor general's report on the Toombs County floggings reported the horrific ordeal of the anti-Klan lawyer Wimberly Brown, who was grabbed on a street corner in the town of Lyons, taken two miles into the woods, his head covered with a sack, and beaten with leather straps: "During pauses, [his assailants] . . . asked him for the name of the reporter who wrote the article which the Macon Telegraph carried about December 6."

The hooded men then promised the semi-conscious Brown that they would " 'get' the Telegraph reporter." The Toombs County stories drew threats of firebombing down on the *Telegraph*, and death threats against Johnson himself mounted to the point that Georgia's governor, Clifford Walker, felt compelled to offer the young man sanctuary, as well as giving notice in strong yet politically careful language that "mobs with heads covered with flour sacks shall not rule in Georgia." (Nathan Bedford Forrest, head of the Klan in Georgia and grandson of the Confederate hero and founder, blamed the whippings on a group of copycat robed "bootleggers and moonshiners.")

The Toombs County stories were the kind of crusading work that might have pleased Johnson's late anti-Klan father, but the experience also proved a valuable test for a young journalist who would later be threatened with death by big-city mobsters. After the success of the Klan series, the *Telegraph*'s editor Ethridge contacted his old friends at the *Sun* about Johnson, with the idea, according to Haynes Johnson, of seasoning his young reporter for an eventual return to Georgia as editor of the *Telegraph*. Two months after starting work in New York, Johnson married a transplanted Macon girl named Ludie Adams.

He began his *Sun* career on the graveyard shift, or "Lobster Trick," "rewriting stories from the morning papers in the quiet predawn hours." One longtime crime reporter, Charles E. Still, had covered the Tombs and big trials starting in the gaslit age, but had since settled very comfortably into a boozy existence running the late shift at the city desk, between visits to his nearby favorite bars along Chambers Street. "More than once, on late rewrite," Johnson wrote, "I would complain of not feeling well, and Charlie would say in a conspiratorial tone: 'Go across the street and catch a couple. I'll watch out for you.'" Later, Still became the large writer of the *Sun*'s bicycle column. "He was old and tremendously fat and very boozy," remembered the *Sun*'s Millie Branham. "But he was kind and friendly, and in the afternoon he was *very* friendly."

But the paper's aging star when Mike arrived was a dandified holdover named Ed Hill, who carried a cane and dressed in spats, striped trousers, and a formal dark coat, and drew on his own florid imagination to give his stories their signature vivacity. Hill, whose account of the sinking of the *Titanic* was still celebrated, was given the duty of rewriting one of Johnson's early efforts, about the latest attempted killing of Jack "Legs" Diamond, known also as "the clay pigeon of the Underworld" for having absorbed so many previous shootings. Johnson's matter-of-fact story for the first edition "got him to the hospital on a stretcher," he recalled, but in Hill's amplified rewrite, "I was amazed to read only in the *Sun* that from his bed of pain Gangster Diamond had snarled epithets that never got snarled by him or anybody else." The veteran Hill had no doubt gambled that Diamond would die of his wounds before he could disclaim Hill's flights of fancy. He didn't.

For Johnson, it was a powerful lesson in old-fashioned showmanship over modern reporting. Many of the events Johnson would cover over the next two decades were hyperbolic enough in themselves without primping by a showboat like Ed Hill, and they would have floated surreally off the page without the anchor of an absolutely sure, fact-gathering witness. By the spring of 1948, Johnson was himself the *Sun*'s longtime veteran star; at forty-three, he was the same age his father had been at his death. Johnson had already lived a full career as a reporter and might naturally have been expected to move on to an editor's desk.

Millie Branham met Mike Johnson after coming to the *Sun* from the potato fields of rural Maine when she was nineteen and was still named Millie Falk. After lightening her hair with lemon juice for her interview, she landed a job as a secretary in the "Woman's Day" department, where her occasional reporting for her overburdened boss eventually brought a visit from Mr. Speed. "One day Mr. Speed comes in and he leans on the door there and he says, 'How would you like to work out in the city room?'" For a young woman, the city room had its hazards—the Argentinian cartoonist Rafael would pause each day as he marched his finished drawing to the editor, put his purple mottled nose close to Millie's ear, and growl, "I will give you a Spanish fly."

While putting her in the path of lecherous cartoonists, her move up also placed Millie Falk on the rewrite bank facing one of the paper's glamorous "byline guys," Mike Johnson, whom she watched pound out stories on his Underwood "with thumb and forefinger of both hands, very hard and very fast, and he'd punish that thing beyond belief." Johnson was one of the paper's "big shots," but also "had this gentle Southern style to him," she remembered; "he called his wife 'Miss Ludie.' It was Mike who named me 'Miss Millie,' and I'm Miss Millie to this day." Once, when Mike took the young Millie Falk on a tour of his favorite nightspots from his stint as a nightclub reporter, "He had to get special permission from Miss Ludie."

By 1948, the *Sun* was a gentlemanly paper on the decline in both readership and ad inches sold. It had fallen down to eighth in circulation among Manhattan's nine dailies, and its nearest political competitor, the conservative *Telegram*, beat it handily. Despite its admired sports and general news departments, the once-great *Sun* was padded with separate columns on antiques, cats, dogs, and tropical fish. The paper had slowed under the ownership of the press lord Frank Munsey, and it never roared as loudly afterward. In readership, political outlook, journalistic style, and office decorum it remained pretty close to where Munsey had left it in 1925, a paper from Coolidge-era America with flashes of its old fire. But it was a combination of the paper's weaknesses and strengths that would allow it to take one of its inspired risks.

Thursday was typically payday in the city room, when the legmen, or district men, who called in stories all week to the rewrite desk came in from their crime scenes and jury watches and bridge jumpers to collect their envelopes. Millie Falk enjoyed meeting the older district men she knew from the phone, such as the one who called in to report how beautifully "built" a slain young actress had looked on the crime scene floor.

On this particular Thursday in April, the city editor, Ed Bartnett, read a report of an incident in northern Manhattan from that morning that he thought echoed a similar crime related to the waterfront in Greenwich Village the year before. If handled by the right reporter, an investigation might get at the possible links and wider causes of these dock wars.

For this bit of digging along the waterfront, Bart did not go to a crime-beat writer, although it was a crime story; nor did he assign a maritime reporter to interrupt his round of boat christenings and steamer arrivals. Instead, he called over his best general assignment man, who had done a powerful series on the national epidemic of truck hijacking just the year before. When Johnson walked across the city room that spring day, he found Bart holding that morning's fresh report. "Lots of unrest down there," the veteran editor told his ace, meaning the waterfront. "Why don't you take a look? Maybe you can get a story out of it."

Mike Johnson got his hat.

CHAPTER 3

BROAD DAYLIGHT

When Mike Johnson reached the pier gates, a group of forty detectives was fanned out along the riverfront, quizzing dockers as they went, their investigation radiating out from West Fifty-second Street. The men named in Bart's report had all worked at West Side Pier 92, one of the Midtown finger piers where hulking passenger ships berthed along Luxury Liner Row. Its beaten-gunmetal sheds ran three hundred yards into the river to accommodate the lordly steamers. Johnson fell in with the detectives and began taking notes in the language of the working waterfront, observing the checkers who tallied freight and the classes of longshoremen who lugged and stowed it; the hatch bosses who oversaw the holdmen, and the public loaders who charged truckers to handle their cargo.

Until this morning, April 29, 1948, this had been Thomas Collentine's pier. He was thirty years old and making at least two hundred dollars per week as a hiring boss, with rich bookmaking and hiring graft at stake beyond the straight dock work he doled out.

Leased to the Atlantic, Gulf, and West Indies Steamship Corporation, Pier 92 was what the DA's office called a "hot" pier, part of a
racket-prone center of passenger shipping controlled both officially
(through its powerful local union delegate, Harold Bowers) and
unofficially (through his mobster cousin Mickey) by the Bowers
gang. The Bowers cousins' dockside ventures included a front
organization called the Allied Stevedoring Company, which gave
them legal access to kickback and truck-loading schemes along the
West Side. Collentine had been hiring boss for nearly two years,
advancing from longie to hatch boss to boss stevedore, but in
recent weeks he had grudgingly shared hiring duties with a rival stevedore installed by the Bowers gang. While detectives
got skimpy answers from the dockers now on shift, they quickly
concluded that what had happened to Collentine that morning
stemmed from a turf war.

Around seven thirty, Collentine had left his three-room apartment in the Inwood section at the northern end of Manhattan to
drive two longshoremen friends down to the pier. As always, he
said goodbye to his wife, Mary, and their two children, walked
down the five flights, and emerged onto Post Avenue. His usual
morning passengers, John White and George Courchesne, were
there to meet him, but when they noticed Collentine's left front tire
was slashed and flat, the three men resolved to walk to the nearby
subway station at Dyckman Street.

No sooner had the trio set out than a large black Buick sedan
appeared, and a gunman wearing a gray suit leaped from the car's
rear door holding a handkerchief across his face and fired seven
times with a .45-caliber automatic. The first volley of four bullets
veered wide and pierced a nearby wall as Collentine and his
friends hit the ground. The gunman then approached, stood over
Collentine, and fired three close shots down into him as he lay on
the pavement. A nearby building super out watering the sidewalk

at the time described the stranger as roughly five foot eight and 160 pounds. As the shooter ran back to the black Buick, the few witnesses spied two accomplices hunkered inside. No one could read the license plate on the car as it lurched off. By the time Mary Collentine had made her way from her kitchen up to the roof, she saw her husband lying down below in the street, all but dead.

"Police today were pursuing a theory that the slaying stemmed from a fight for the control of lucrative gambling rackets," Johnson reported on page 1 of the *Sun* the day after the killing. Bowers's replacement stevedore was clapped into the Tombs for questioning, and Collentine's two friends who had escaped that morning's stray bullets were held as material witnesses for their own protection. The story headline claimed that the shooting was "patterned" on the recent murder of another hiring boss, Anthony "Andy" Hintz, in 1947. But unlike Hintz or Peter Panto, whose defiance eventually cost them their lives, Thomas Collentine had begun as a cooperative man of the system, a usefully brawny enforcer rewarded with a longshore union job. As Johnson noted, Collentine had himself "been questioned in connection with three waterfront killings since 1943." His fatal grievance came over his own stake in waterfront rackets such as payroll padding and the usurious loading fees at his pier—not against gang influence itself. With him lying gut-shot that morning outside his apartment house, the killing concluded a weeks-long struggle.

Maritime reporting largely ignored the criminal side in favor of chronicling the arrivals of important people on liners; the reporter typically made his way by cutter to the incoming steamship for photos and questions before the starlet or other notable made official landfall. According to Johnson's friend at the *Sun* Robert Wilder, who'd enjoyed his share of Cunard scotch through the years, it was "the softest of all berths a newspaper has to offer." Johnson wasn't a specialist in waterfront affairs, but "there was no one else that we had free who could handle these things," remembered his city room colleague Millie Branham. "Mike was on his own."

Johnson knew that killings such as Collentine's were dispiritingly familiar around the harbor. Like most New Yorkers, he knew the docks could be a rough, even deadly place, but he had only a general suspicion about the waterfront rackets behind the killings. To learn more, you had to put in time closer to shore—moving cargo, policing a riverfront beat, or covering territorial skirmishes. According to the district attorney's office, several dozen waterfront murders had gone unsolved over the twenty years leading up to the Collentine shooting. Assistant DA William J. Keating, who knew the West Side docks then, described the bleak outlook for waterfront prosecutions:

> Waterfront murders were the most hopeless of cases. Longshoremen were always getting shot, or beaten over the head with baseball bats, or flung into the harbor. There seldom was any real mystery about the killings. The murderers were usually well known but arrests and convictions were unheard of, because waterfront workers and their families had little confidence in cops and talked to them only off the record, if at all. A man could be killed in broad daylight before half a dozen witnesses and nobody would testify about it. On the waterfront, to talk was to rat, and to rat was to stand exposed and unprotected.

Johnson would grow frustrated at how these bloody set pieces were rarely linked in the press. In the early morning of December 9, 1939, David Beadle entered a Tenth Avenue bar and grill called the Spot long enough to ask for a glass of water and swallow a pill. When he emerged and turned south at the corner of West Forty-sixth Street a taxi drew up. Several men stepped from the cab and shot Beadle in the head, then drove off. "The Beetle," as he had been known along the West Side docks, turned out to be not only a stevedore and pier boss but also a former bootlegger involved in loan-sharking and "policy" games on the piers— "a longshoremen's racket," said a detective.

Past eleven on the night of April 23, 1940, months after one of them had been questioned and released in the shooting death of David Beadle, two longshoremen, the brothers James and Vincent Doherty, were eating sandwiches in a drugstore on Tenth Avenue and Fifty-first Street. A gunman entered the place and fired into their booth six times before escaping into a car. Vincent Doherty was wounded in the side, but the older brother, James, was hit in the head and died within thirty-five minutes.

Richard "the Bandit" Gregory was eating lunch in the Hudson Hofbräu on Twelfth Avenue near Forty-fifth Street, a place the Bandit frequently visited to collect union dues and other payments, when his killer found him on the afternoon of November 16, 1940. While Gregory's dozen arrests included three for homicide, he was a delegate in ILA Local 824, called the "Pistol Local" for its murderous history, and a prosperous manager of waterfront enterprises from loan-sharking to pierside betting. Gregory was shot four times while standing at the Hofbräu's bar, and reached desperately into his pocket to retrieve his union card, which he flashed at either his assailant or the bartender witness as he sank. "Here," he sighed, before sagging to the floor. Detectives "sought to determine whether his union background or his criminal record figured in the attack," the *Times* reporter summarized. As his dying flourish made clear, it was both.

In December 1944, nearly five years after the death of "the Beetle" and only yards from his murder site at Forty-sixth Street and Tenth Avenue, Beadle's former business partner in a stevedoring firm, Tommy Gleason, was shot dead as he napped in the reception room of a funeral home. Only weeks before, Gleason had attacked Mickey Bowers, whom he held responsible for Beadle's death, slashing at his throat with a knife, then fleeing. About the funeral parlor shooter who'd put the gun to the dozing Gleason's head, witnesses were typically mum.

So the waterfront murders came and went, acts of score settling or territorial consolidation, against a whispery background of labor "troubles," longshore rackets, and gang rivalries. The initial reports were often studded with the sayings of guardedly hopeful detectives, but rarely was one event tied to others in the press, and given the reluctance of so many witnesses, few cases reached trial. "Most such murders go unsolved," Johnson wrote. "The harbor police fish bodies of dead men out of the river and list them as victims of gang warfare on the docks."

What Johnson knew about how rackets functioned he'd learned from his recent investigation of the national boom in truck hijacking, which by his reckoning stole roughly $25 million in merchandise in 1947 alone. Like a scientist watching ants bear away a picnic, Johnson traced the fate of heisted goods from the initial targeting by networks of "finger men" to the work of "spotters," who passed the information on to hijacking crews, followed by the crucial unloading of stolen textiles, furs, or liquor through fences, with the gang's bondsmen bailing out anyone caught in the robbery. One accomplished New York fence Johnson found, "a pudgy, dark, middle-aged man whose 'front' is a retail store on the lower East Side," kept no telephone but received his calls nearby, where

If his conversation with the gang leader should by chance be overheard it would sound like an innocent social call:

"Hello," says the gang leader, addressing the fence by his nickname.

"How's everything with you?"

"OK," replies the fence. "What are you doing?"

"I got a date to do a little shopping with my girl friend. I'm going to try to buy her some nylons."

This is the tipoff that the hijacker has a load of stockings.

Pier 92 became the entry point through which Johnson fitfully, methodically found his way to the sweeping picture Pete Panto had described a decade earlier—of a New York waterfront dominated by a loose alliance of shipping and gangster interests, with a powerful longshoremen's union increasingly indistinguishable from the racketeers. A decade after the Panto killing, he could still feel the palpable fear among longshoremen.

All that spring of 1948, Johnson struggled with his waterfront crime story, a gracious, softly drawling stranger in a reporter's suit trying to ingratiate himself with the men shaping at the pierheads or taking their ease in longie bars between whistles. More often than not he met with the dockers' traditional mistrust toward investigators, their defensive pose of "D and D" (deaf and dumb). The men's shrugging answers were little different from those they'd given to Rackets Bureau men or waterfront detectives before him. Even for dying men, it turned out, a spiteful silence was the accepted style: "I don't know who shot me," Thomas Collentine had snapped at detectives with perverse loyalty to code, "and if I did I wouldn't tell you." Eleven hours after being shot, he died in Jewish Memorial Hospital in Inwood without talking about his killers in the dark sedan.

For six frustrating weeks Johnson could not break through the dockers' defense, let alone begin to identify the full criminal terrain beneath his feet. As he sat in waterfront bars, he knew the heavy silence of so many of the men hinted at a wider story he could not grasp. He could take some comfort in the true struggles of another newsman who'd faced a wall of silence, the *Chicago*

Sun-Times reporter P. J. McNeal, played by Jimmy Stewart in *Call Northside 777*, which opened the week of Johnson's first disorienting visits to the docks. The Chicago Police Department closed ranks against McNeal's investigation much like Johnson was experiencing with the longies on the West Side. The key to both cases was turning up the first unexpected informant who'd crack the silence.

"Several times I was almost ready to give up, convinced that the real story never would be uncovered," Johnson later admitted. "Then I had some lucky breaks: One was meeting and gaining the confidence of an informant, an ex-convict, who had worked with the racketeers. His story set the pattern, and he steered me to other sources." An old acquaintance who had since left the FBI heard rumors of Johnson's stalled investigation and got him in touch with a man Johnson would later identify only as "Joe." The informant was perfectly placed to be Johnson's guide, having known life in the union and the waterfront gangs but with no remaining connection to either.

"Joe" had been "a member of the Bowers gang until he was accused of 'crossing up the boys' and marked for quick extermination." After surviving one attempt on his life, he entered protective custody. Johnson described meeting Joe in "a small seedy hotel where he was registered under an assumed name." Joe told Johnson his story, starting with his time at Sing Sing for robbery in the early thirties, when he met an inmate serving for burglary named Johnny Applegate:

> We got friendly . . . He was getting out before I did and he told me to look him up when I got out. I got out in January 1938, and some months later I looked up Apple on the waterfront. He introduced me to a union delegate they called the Bandit, who got me a union membership book without me having to pay for it. I got steady

work as a longshoreman with that book, though I never had done a day's work on the waterfront in my life. I soon got to know all the ins and outs, and how the rackets worked. With Apple's help, I did all right.

The man who had given Joe his union book, the ILA delegate Richard "the Bandit" Gregory, died standing at the bar of the Hudson Hofbräu in November 1940, trying to show his union card to his killer. Joe made clear how unsubtle a business it was to take over a pier. Following the death of the Bandit, he explained, "there was another fight for power on the Upper West Side. A new mob walked in and took over. That was the Bowers mob, and I started paying dues to those boys." The new collector of dues was Harold Bowers, "who became the union delegate for Local 824 after the Bandit was bumped off."

At the time Johnson wrote Joe's story, it ended when he later skipped town chased by a Mob vendetta, shipping out on a tanker. In real life, though, Joe was almost certainly a man named Dominick Genova, who several years later told the New York State Crime Commission an identical story of his rise and fall on the West Side. Genova's story was typical of a waterfront pattern in those days of convicts meeting useful mentors while at prison and being hired right onto the docks upon release. Genova's debt of friendship, he found, only grew with his job responsibilities: he rose from baggage handling for the *Queen Mary* to collecting horse and numbers bets in a cigar box on the piers, graduated to a position as a checker, and was finally asked to return his many favors by committing a murder for one of his bosses. When Genova ungratefully turned down the job, he was "marked 'lousy' " and fled the waterfront.

Genova knew the Bowers organization well and had even been present when his docks rival Tommy Gleason slashed the throat of

Mickey Bowers in front of a West Side bar and grill in 1944: "It seemed like Gleason was going to pat him on the cheek, but he had a knife in his hand and he cut him in the throat," Genova told the Crime Commission. "Bowers grabbed his throat, turned around and ran inside the bar, and Gleason jumped in a cab and ran away. . . . I think it was a week or two later, [Gleason] was murdered in an undertaking parlor, sitting there having a snooze." "Joe," or Genova, "set the pattern" for Johnson's later investigation, and sketched out a broad map whose criminal details would have taken the reporter months more to puzzle out on his own.

Johnson's second break followed in early summer. William J. Keating was the descendant of three generations of Pennsylvania coal miners back to his great-grandfather, Mountain Jim Keating, an Irish immigrant and member of the militant miner group the Molly Maguires. Bill Keating had escaped the mines to become a scrappily sincere young prosecutor in the Homicide Bureau of the Manhattan district attorney's office. He had dedicated himself to gathering an impressive sheaf on waterfront crime, an area that inspired caution in many prosecutors for its low rate of convictions and dearth of cooperative witnesses. The murder of the pugnacious dock boss Anthony Hintz in January 1947, though noted by only one paper initially, grew into a landmark case in waterfront crime through a series of highly unusual events: most important, the victim actually broke ranks and named his killer (docks racketeer John "Cockeye" Dunn); then the case was fearlessly prosecuted by a young assistant DA before he died; and, finally, rather than Mob intimidation squelching the case for "lack of evidence," the assailants were resoundingly convicted.

Keating and Johnson met at a fortunate juncture for both. Keating was fresh from the sensational achievement of the Dunn case and needed outlets to keep sounding his anti-rackets message, while Johnson was hungry for sources with access to credible information. Few along the waterfront would talk to Johnson at the time he met Keating, who, despite his recent success, was getting pressured by his bosses in the DA's office to tone down his own waterfront probe. The Dunn conviction had not led to the larger "crackdown on the piers" Keating had hoped for, but was followed instead by a return to caution, in which each pier crime was considered on its own. He sought to make the connection Bill O'Dwyer had stopped short of making as Brooklyn DA, between gang murders and the waterfront's spoils system.

The murder of Thomas Collentine seemed to Keating to be a textbook "planned assassination" on the model of the Hintz killing. He told this to every reporter he met in the hopes that someone would dig into it. "As with the Hintz murder," Keating recalled in his tough, fluent memoir, *The Man Who Rocked the Boat*, "important elements in the police department did not find my enthusiasm contagious, and many of my own colleagues grew cool . . . [T]he waterfront spelled trouble and nobody with an adequately developed sense of the political expedience of things wanted to mess with the dock rackets any more than absolutely necessary."

Unfazed, in the weeks following Collentine's death, Keating rudely dragged Harold and Mickey Bowers into the office not once but several times for questioning. Harold Bowers had recently become business agent in the North River's notorious "Pistol Local," number 824, to which Collentine had belonged since he was sixteen. "My visits with Mickey Bowers and his large cousin Harold were amusing, if uninformative," Keating wrote. When Harold Bowers angrily demanded Keating name the alleged mobsters on his waterfront, "I answered with a review of Mickey's career, including the time he took a seven-and-a-half-to-fifteen-year rap for a payroll robbery in which Harold himself had been implicated but cleared. I mentioned the gamy records of the murderers and armed bandits who worked as hiring bosses in Harold's own fiefdom." When the young lawyer had finished his lecture, Harold Bowers grinned, "lifted his hands and shrugged. 'Look,' he said. 'I got no time for this crap. I gotta go uptown to take my elocution lesson.' "

After Mickey Bowers's latest visit to the undeferential young prosecutor, the ILA's president, Joe Ryan, complained to Keating's boss, DA Frank Hogan. Continuing to question his union leaders would "sabotage the wage-scale negotiations" then ongoing, Ryan claimed, and could threaten a portwide strike. "It has been reported to me by one of our International representatives . . . that District Attorney Keating of your staff is summonising many of them down to his office for questioning regarding conditions on the waterfront, and upon leaving they are informed that they shall be called down again." Hogan was impressed enough by Ryan's grievance that the two drafted a private agreement stating that no ILA officer could be questioned without Ryan's clearance. It was in the midst of this frustration, as Keating was struggling to sell his campaign against the dock rackets both inside the office and outside to the press, that he heard that "something more exciting" had happened: "Morty Davis, criminal courts reporter for the New York *Sun*, said that his city editor had assigned the paper's ace, Malcolm Johnson, to do a piece or two on the Collentine case." It was Bill Keating's chance to deliver his message, even if he had to sneak around his politic boss and light a fire under him in the press to do it.

Morty Davis arranged a meeting between the two men, at which Keating first told Johnson that because of libel considerations for living witnesses, he could not discuss an active case such as Collentine's. There were, however, "other possibilities." According to Keating, he next mentioned the previous year's Hintz murder, for which the three killers were then awaiting execution at Sing Sing. Keating clearly sensed a kindred spirit in Johnson, someone as passionate and uncynical about corruption as he was. The Bowers gang Johnson had been researching in the Collentine drama was small stuff, Keating assured him, compared with the downtown racketeers of the Dunn-McGrath mob. "The Dunn mob was more important than those Bowers people and used to treat them like servants." Beyond that, Keating offered, "There is no reason at all why you can't go through the Dunn case file. You'll be the first newspaperman to do it and I'm sure you'll pick up a lot of interesting material."

CHAPTER 4

JOHNNY SHOT ME

The Dunn files now sit among many other overstuffed boxes of dead cases in a warehouse near the Brooklyn waterfront. If you put in a call slip, a truck brings them out of the past and over the bridge to the wooden tables of the Municipal Archives, down the block on Chambers Street from the mounted clocks of the old Sun Building. It is easy to understand Mike Johnson's quick fascination with the world he encountered when he untied these bulging green-brown folders packed with police reports, death house confessions, lawyers' trial jottings, lists of hit men's phone calls ("Gus & Andy's Restaurant & Bar, CH 4-9156"), onionskin transcripts, and a gangster's vacation photos and letters to his daughter. A homicide detective's report summarizes the clear motive behind a West Village shooting ("deceased would not allow the defendants to dictate to him as to whom he should employ on Pier 51, north river . . ."); there are long institutional narratives of the shooters, a lab description of the holes and stains to the dead man's raincoat, and a mimeographed anatomy drawing marked with his bullet tracks.

This collection of now-yellowing documents was part of a crash course for Johnson; the contents of these files broadened his story from the killing of one foreman on a single "hot" pier to one alleging a national crime syndicate. After his weeks of meeting silence as he toured the docks, Johnson suddenly had leads in a hundred directions. According to Bill Keating, after learning what the DA had gathered on the Dunn and Bowers gangs, Johnson "became so interested in the material that he got permission to do a series on waterfront crime." More dock sources would follow—a loan shark named Johnny Clinton, a boss loader named Slivers Thompson, other "underworld informers" code-named "Nick" or "John Berg." Another of Ed Bartnett's hunches was panning out, perhaps more spectacularly than he realized. The Hintz case he had been reminded of from 1947 turned out to hold the key to a much bigger story.

The redbrick apartment house at 61 Grove Street in the West Village was topped with gape-mouthed gargoyles, shared its short block with a long-lived piano bar, and sat beside a weathered plaque marking the birth and death of Thomas Paine. Andy Hintz, a forty-three-year-old boss stevedore, lived in apartment 3A. Hintz oversaw some 200 to 250 men of his own choosing each day at nearby Pier 51, at the foot of Jane Street, and at about 7:40 on the morning of January 8, 1947, he started down the three flights on his way to work.

Three men in long coats and fedoras had preceded him into his hallway by several minutes. Stalking across the rooftops through tangles of cold laundry that flapped in the breeze off the river, they entered Hintz's building by the roof door, made their way down to the second-floor landing, and tensely waited. Like figures out of a

Dick Tracy comic, they were a motley trio: a racketeer widely known as "Cockeye" had brought along both a professional killer (Andrew Sheridan), so near-blind himself from a childhood dousing with caustic acid that he was nicknamed Squint, and a numbers runner and former boxer, Danny Gentile, who carried no gun. The crew lay in wait for Andy Hintz.

Since his appointment as hiring boss the previous November, Hintz had resisted the encroachment of Johnny Dunn, now thirty-six, whose off-kilter right eye moved people to privately call him "Cockeye." Reporters summed up Dunn further as "runty," while Mike Johnson saw him as a "wiry little Irishman." After finishing a short term at Sing Sing for robbing a card game, Dunn discovered the waterfront in the mid-1930s. Together with his hoodlum partner (and future brother-in-law) Eddie McGrath, Dunn secured charters from both the ILA and the American Federation of Labor to form his own union locals, even founding a union for terminal checkers and platform men to infiltrate the loading side. These successes allowed the Dunn-McGrath group to add the strike threat to its means of extortion, and to transform something called Varick Enterprises into what the reporter Allen Raymond described as "a collection agency for boss loaders along the docks. . . . The collections were enforced by goons armed with guns or blackjacks. Truckmen paid under threat of violence to have their trucks unloaded."

A convict named Buster Smith, who had been shot by the Dunn-McGrath gang on two different occasions, laid out for Johnson a typically bloody account of Johnny Dunn's relentlessness in claiming territory along the docks, involving shootings in three boroughs to secure the loading on a single Manhattan pier:

In 1936 . . . me and George Keeler and Tom Porter had the loading at Pier 59 at 18th Street. Dunn's gang was trying to get bigger control, and they just moved in on us. Dunn and his boys opened up on us one day with pistols and shotguns. I was wounded. A few weeks later, Dunn, Matty Kane, and some others killed Tom Porter and his girl in Long Island City. Tom and his girl were sitting in an automobile. They killed her because they didn't want no witnesses, I guess. A month later Dunn and two of his gunmen knocked off George Keeler at his home in Brooklyn. They shot George as he was asleep in his bed. With me wounded and Keeler and Porter dead, Dunn's boys took over our loading at Pier 59.

One of the Dunn victims, George Keeler, was killed in his upstairs bedroom while sleeping beside his wife, who was jolted half awake by the shots but decided she was still dreaming about the gangster movie the couple had seen that night. In April 1941, after serving a sentence for violation of parole, Buster Smith was released and quickly shot a second time, in a bar and grill, by a trio that included Cockeye Dunn and Andrew Sheridan, who had killed together many times along the docks before going to visit Andy Hintz.

"The function of Dunn," wrote the man who finally prosecuted him, Bill Keating, "was to maintain order among what very likely was the most disorganized and heavily exploited industrial labor force in the United States, the longshoremen." By 1946, the Dunn-McGrath gang already controlled hiring and loading on piers south of Fourteenth Street. The galling exception was Pier 51, where Andy Hintz stubbornly hired neighborhood men over Dunn candidates at his shape-ups and refused to cut Dunn in for a share of the loading fees. Dunn's interest in this elusive pier went back at least to the beginning of the war, when he had feuded with another boss stevedore there, Ed Kelly, whom he beat up in a Tenth Street saloon. When this failed to change Kelly's mind, Dunn surrounded his pier with a picket line, hoping to get the stevedore fired as an ineffective manager when loading came to a halt. Instead, Dunn's pickets blocked a British ship from joining two wartime convoys, and Dunn was sent to prison for coercion. Hintz was installed over Dunn's candidate, a man called "Ding Dong" Bell, after wartime controls ended in 1946, and the stalking of Hintz began—cars regularly trailed him and jiggled their lights when he drove. Then, according to witnesses, Danny Gentile appeared on the pier one workday afternoon to deliver an offer from his boss: Hintz could keep control if he would "play ball" and share hiring privileges with Dunn. As one Hintz friend later told prosecutors, "Andy chased the rat. He hollered at him so that a couple hundred men could hear, 'Tell that cockeyed son of a bitch to go to hell . . .' " Hintz's message was received.

Crouched above Dunn that morning in that Grove Street stairway was Andy "Squint" Sheridan, a large, crisply dressed, jowly gunman with blue eyes and thick glasses. Sheridan had at one time been a member of the Dutch Schultz beer gang. The DA's files on the Dunn case are leavened with souvenir photos of Sheridan seated happily among a ring of friends in places such as the Ha-Ha Club. It is hard to imagine this heavy, bespectacled man as the same one who would later assure prosecutors that killing was "just as easy as ordering a cup of coffee." Like Dunn, he had risen from petty larceny and holdups to assault and murder, and moved from the Catholic protectories to the state penitentiary system. "Squint" Sheridan had once shot the wrong man, but on the night of February 7, 1941, he walked onto a West Side pier and asked four men loading a truck, "Who's Moran?" just to be sure. "I am," answered Sheridan's mark in the half-darkness, and Squint shot him. On assignment a month later, he killed another docker, John "The Mutt" Whitton, in a toilet on Pier 14, North River. Then, according to state records, he somehow "stuffed his body down the drain."

Danny Gentile, the former boxer who fought as Danny Brooks

and who rounded out the trio that morning, had been convicted for "possession of policy slips" for a pier lottery in 1941, and was the Dunn messenger Hintz had so loudly chased off his pier. Though hardly a killer himself, Gentile turned out to be the fatal go-between in the feud. (Dunn later claimed that had he meant to kill Hintz that day, he never would have brought along someone as weak-minded and chatty as Gentile.)

The three ambushers crouched in the hallway. Hintz had just kissed his wife goodbye and was moving down the stairs when the men appeared at the next landing. "Kill the rat cocksucker!" Hintz remembered Dunn screaming just before the shots. "Kill him and kill the rat cocksucker brother of his!" But Dunn would have to do all the shooting—five times into the stevedore's thick body—after Sheridan's gun jammed. To prove his worth, Danny Gentile, who carried no gun that day, got in a couple of kicks to Hintz's head and face as he lay on the stairs.

Outside, Hintz's brother Willie and a driver sat out front in a Ford sedan waiting to make the short ride to the pier. Willie sat in the Ford's rear seat reading the paper while the driver rang the doorbell. Willie Hintz did not hear the shots when they came but recognized the ex-fighter Danny Brooks (Gentile) in a brown coat running from the building and toward Seventh Avenue.

Inside, Hintz's wife heard the gunfire and ran out in her bathrobe. Hintz was calling upstairs for her, a neighbor told detectives. "Who did it?" Maisie shouted back. "Johnny shot me," said Hintz. Maisie Hintz found her husband lying facedown on the stairs. "Dunn, Dunn," he moaned, having taken five bullets in the gut, chest, and face. After neighbors carried him back upstairs to the apartment's bathroom, Maisie Hintz sponged blood from his face and begged her husband to repeat who had done it. "Johnny Dunn shot me."

Dunn and Sheridan escaped to the roof and crossed to an

adjoining building on Christopher Street, where they had first entered that morning. Mrs. Josephine Lopez, who lived with her four children on the top floor of 78 Christopher, was just rising when she heard men's footsteps that "came from farther away at first and grew louder . . . I went out in the hall—it was light because the roof door was open." When she went up she saw no sign of anyone, except by the roof door the men had used there was a puddle of urine.

By the time Hintz reached St. Vincent's Hospital, the waterfront code had set in like a kind of rigor mortis. For three days he denied Dunn was involved, insisted he had been shot instead by a mysterious man in a gray overcoat, hat, and sweater. "What's the use of saying he done it when he didn't?" Hintz replied to investigators at his bedside. "If it was him I would tell you, Cap." Over the weeks he lingered in the hospital he gave several different "dying declarations" to a court stenographer. Then, on the morning of January 11, after being convinced by a friend who was a waterfront cop that his wife and brother would remain in danger after his death, Hintz named his attackers. Dunn, dressed much as he had been in the hallway, was brought to the foot of Hintz's hospital bed for the identification and did his genial best to intimidate the dying witness who was bucking the code:

DUNN: You know you and I never had any difference in the world.

HINTZ: Not much.

DUNN: Did we have any, Andy?

HINTZ: Not much, we didn't.

DUNN: Tell the truth here, will you please?

HINTZ: I told the truth.

DUNN: (Removing hat) Take another look at me. I hope you are all right. Are you rational?

When Dunn asked again if Hintz was "satisfied you are telling the truth," Hintz, who was a mess of tubes and exit tracks, bitterly shouted, "Yes, that's right. Son-of-a-bitch, if I—" and began tearing at his hospital gown to "show him where I got it" and "see if he is satisfied" with the wounds on his stomach and chest. Hintz's final declaration to prosecutors, in answer to the question "Who fired the shots at you?" ("Dunn. He done well too"), came after he'd been given last rites three times, and made possible the first-degree murder case. But even after naming his assailants, Hintz asked the DA's men sheepishly if they thought he was a "rat."

Dunn had fired every shot in that hallway after Squint's gun jammed, a mechanical failure that Dunn would bitterly blame for their prosecution. If all chambers had been working that day, he later told a prison snitch, nothing would have come out of Andy Hintz's mouth. ("Cockeye did it," the Hintz-like rebel boss moans after he's shot on the stairs in *Slaughter on Tenth Avenue*, the film adapted from Bill Keating's account of the Dunn case, "Cockeye and two of his meatballs.")

By the late spring of 1948, when Mike Johnson got his privileged look at the Hintz case, Dunn, Sheridan, and Gentile were on death row at Sing Sing, waiting on several appeals. The two pier murders, those of Collentine and Hintz, showed Johnson the central importance of the shape-up and of who controlled it. If he came to see much of the waterfront as an "outlaw frontier," he saw the shape-up as the main source of the outlaws' power over the men who worked the docks.

Just as Bill Keating's investigation had run afoul of the longshore union, word of Mike Johnson's reporting soon disturbed the ILA's president, Joe Ryan.

CHAPTER 5

KING JOE

Joseph Patrick Ryan had risen pretty far on his aggressive charm, and if he thought of his union and himself as one and the same, the confusion would have been understandable, since they had come of age together. During his two decades in office, "President for Life" Ryan liked to hammishly say the initials of his International Long-shoremen's Association really stood for "I Love America." As a young man he'd been a redheaded battler for the emerging ILA, but Ryan was now a graying, bushy-browed man of sixty-eight whose blue serge suits and vivid ties covered a powerfully blocky build. "I like good food of all kinds and I think my longshoremen want me to have it," he unwisely told a reporter during the wartime rationing. The most he asked of his body these days was a round of nine at Mamaroneck's Winged Foot Golf Club, but the dents across his knuckles hinted at his exertions in past labor wars.

Ryan liked to begin most days with a review of his laboring troops. Leaving his Chelsea apartment after breakfast with his wife,

Maggie, he walked to Guardian Angel Church for the eight o'clock Mass as the whistles sounded and the clumps of dockers who toed the cobbles for the shape-up were falling into work gangs. After Mass, he continued downtown in a singing mood (especially if a reporter trailed him) along the stretch of Hudson called the North River, toward union headquarters—watching the early crowd claiming tables inside the boozeless oddity, The Longshoremen's Rest, then greeting winchmen and cargo handlers and smelling the freshly landed spices at the deepwater piers, passing the human line of "banana fiends" handing bunches ashore at the fruit docks. He hailed veteran dockers by name and nodded beneficently to the flophouse drifters called shenangoes, who picked up small jobs for drink money. Ryan was known to give out five-dollar bills to the sadder cases he met, and to break into misty old ballads such as "Danny Deever" ("For they're hangin' Danny Deever, you can hear the Dead March play / The regiment's in 'ollow square—they're hangin' him to-day") and "When You and I Were Young, Maggie" as he walked. To the romantic ear of the *Times*'s Meyer Berger following along, Joe delivered these melodies "quite smoothly . . . with beery overtones."

With his morning review completed, Ryan turned landward and settled in at his glass-topped desk in the union's offices on West Fourteenth Street, high in the Lawyers' Trust building. From his windows on the nineteenth floor, he could fill out almost any biographical anecdote for a visitor by pointing to the dramatic and sentimental spots from his five decades in the neighborhood—the St. Francis Xavier school he'd left at age twelve to help support his family; the Twenty-third Street trolley young Ryan walked as a conductor; the Chelsea pier where a five-hundred-pound load of lead ingots squelched his brief career as a working longshoreman; the Joseph P. Ryan Association on West Eighteenth Street, where he headed most evenings for fraternal politicking.

Ryan was born to Irish immigrants in Babylon, Long Island, in 1884. His mother, Mary Shanahan, died giving birth to him, and his father, James Ryan, a gardener, remarried before passing away himself within a few years. In Ryan's later interviews and speeches, he saved some of his fiercest tributes for his stepmother, Bridget Meade Ryan. "If I don't lie or swear or smoke," said Ryan, who indulged in all three, "if I'm a churchgoing man, all the credit to her." Leaving their two sisters to live with their uncle, the stepmother brought the Ryan boys to New York City, where nine-year-old Joe began his life in the Irish neighborhood of pubs, churches, and dock labor that would form him: Chelsea. He and his older brother, Thomas, attended Xavier nearby until the family's poverty pushed Joe into work as a stockboy, blanket salesman, and clerk in Lower Manhattan; he joined the Metropolitan Street Railway in 1905, and advanced over seven years from conductor to inspector. "Seeing no future," Ryan later wrote in one of two unfinished memoirs, he joined his brother on the Chelsea docks, where the pay was no better but, he noted, the union was at least growing. He became a dock man on Pier 60, North River.

It was one day in 1912, while working down in the hold of the S.S. *Celtic*, a twenty-one-thousand-ton steamer that traveled the New York–Queenstown–Liverpool route, that Ryan suffered his life-changing accident:

"We were handling pig lead, 25 to a draft," he wrote, "and the gangway man was in a great hurry to get the last draft in. He wanted to rush home to get his oil coat while the gang were shifting inshore to take in oil cake . . . He left, the draft come down too fast and when the pig lead, lashed together by a copper chain, struck the top of the steel tank which we were working in, something had to give . . . the 25 pigs of lead were thrown in on top of us six men."

The falling lead smashed Ryan's shoulder, fracturing the clavicle and laying him up for twelve weeks. It was a rough lesson in

waterfront conditions, where foremen like his were largely un-
accountable for their blunders, unless they affected the ship's
turnaround time in port. Few such accidents were scrutinized to
separate employee foolishness from employer negligence, and not
many longshoremen could afford to take out accident policies, anyway. Although Ryan's injury was all too common on the docks, its
later effect on his career's direction proved unusual.

During this same period, a young man named Charles Barnes,
then a fellow in social research from the New York School of Phi-
lanthropy, was also at work on the docks, compiling an astonish-
ingly thorough and sympathetic study of waterfront workers, *The
Longshoremen*. Barnes investigated everything he could about
dockers' lives—the various nationalities drawn together in the
daily competition of the shape-up, the men's activities during the
long waits between jobs, the variety of skills that distinguished different forms of dock work, the history of wages in the industry, and
the often-disastrous saga of its early unions. Barnes also supplied a
glossary of docker terms he'd encountered: from *ca' canny* (Scots
for "hold back" or "go slow") and *square-heads* (designating Nor-
wegians, Swedes, or Danes) to *boot for shoe* (for reversing ends of a
rope). And the wooden loading bucket known by the men as the
fruit box was swiftly called the *ambulance* in the case of accidents,
when it hauled damaged bodies ashore.

Barnes analyzed as many injuries to longshoremen as he could
verify, through combining often gruesome accounts he got from
dockers themselves with more cryptic hospital, coroner, and state
records. For the months running up to Joe Ryan's mishap in
the hold of the *Celtic* (1910–1911), Barnes could authenticate
309 longshore accidents on the Manhattan waterfront, 96 of them
fatal: "Twenty-eight men were knocked or fell into the hold from
the upper deck; 5 men lost their footing while reaching out with

their hooks from lower decks to pull in a draft and fell to their death; 16 men were hit by swinging drafts with fatal result."

The remaining deaths came from snapped booms, a rolling log, exploding chemical drums; being "dragged into a cog wheel of a winch or pulled around the drum end," knocked by a sling to a lower deck, or crushed by a swinging load. While "leaning over the hatch coamings," one unlucky gangway man had his head cut off by a falling box of tin.

The 213 stories of nonfatal accidents Barnes collected recalled scaldings from the steam-driven winches, plunges from the rigging or into darkened hatchways, fingers lost in the clash of heavy loads, or legs mangled in a draft of mahogany. Barnes's study confirmed that the ship's hold, where Ryan was hurt and where men often relied merely on the rattle of a chain to know if a load was dropping toward them, was the most dangerous place on the waterfront. Yet of the ninety-six deadly injuries he studied, Barnes could verify only five in which compensation was officially paid by the shipping company. Of the nonfatal cases, many of which incapacitated the longshoremen for months or ended their usefulness for dock work altogether, compensation was made more frequently, even if limited to buying the victim a wooden leg. Joe Ryan's treatment was therefore above average for a waterfront injury in 1912; for taking the falling lead that day, he received $350, half of which went to his lawyer.

After he was knocked down in the hold, Ryan was dealt a worse blow during his weeks of convalescence: his young son died of convulsions. On his return to work, Ryan was nominated to fill a vacancy as his local's financial secretary, an honor he attributed mainly "to the fact that I had just come through such an ordeal." Whatever mixture of reasons lay behind the appointment, the position marked the start of his rise in the union.

The growing ILA was overtaking the older Longshoremen's Union Protective Association, which it formally absorbed by 1914. As a young officer under President T. V. O'Connor, Ryan proved a passionate speaker and able brawler during the labor wars of the teens, taking his "boys" on occasional violent errands such as calling on a rebellious Hoboken local's meeting at contract time in the fall of 1919, when Ryan was arrested for possession of firearms. He also showed himself to be a clever tactician in thwarting the challenge made by the Five Points gang leader Paul Vaccarelli, who under the more Irish-sounding name Paul Kelly founded his own short-lived longshore organization in a bid for loading rights. Through well-placed loyalty and political skill, Ryan outlasted his remaining rivals on the waterfront to become the ILA's president by 1927.

The organization he came to run had started on the Great Lakes as an association of coal trimmers, riggers, and lumber handlers. Its first local was established in Chicago in 1877, but its official name was adopted fifteen years later, at a convention in Detroit. Its predecessor unions had fought a series of disastrous wars with the Lumber Carriers' Association, but the ILA's early leaders showed a prowess for deal-making and symbolic concessions long before Ryan made these part of his own style.

But it was his attempt to settle a violent Pacific Coast strike of his longshoremen in 1934 that forced a permanent continental divide in his organization—leaving a radical but effective union under Harry Bridges to fight for West Coast dockers, and Ryan's collection of union toughs and racketeers, the ILA, in the East. Ryan's anticommunism served his political purposes, but the core of it was genuine, based not only in what he'd seen happen to other unions but also in a legitimate fear of Bridges's public ambitions to expand his movement east. "The Nose," as Bridges was known for his familiar beaky profile, had made no secret of his designs on

Ryan's Atlantic ports. Days after Ryan fired him from his position as a Pacific Coast organizer during the Great Strike of 1934, Bridges spoke against Ryan at a rally of twelve thousand in Madison Square Garden financed by the Communist Party. By 1942, when Ryan had himself securely elected "president for life," he made $22,000 per year, with access to numerous other monies, including an anticommunism fund that could be dipped into seemingly whenever he felt a threat to freedom.

Ryan's name came up in nearly all the waterfront talk Mike Johnson was hearing that spring of 1948—as a union dictator, as a tool of the gangsters or the shippers or both. Even an enemy like Bill Keating in the DA's office, who saw Ryan as a "florid, plugugly" figurehead, respected his guile and survival skills. He was a friend of Tammany Hall and of the new mayor, Bill O'Dwyer, a man who as a young cop had seen up close how things worked on the waterfront.

On June 7, just five weeks since the murder that first brought him to the docks, Johnson sat down at his Underwood in the *Sun* city room and pounded out a "Confidential Memo to the City Desk." The subject was Ryan's influence around the harbor. Johnson's five pages of anecdote and accusation were heavily informed by the files shown to him by Bill Keating, and gave his editors a tantalizing summary of the DA's charges about Ryan's "racket background . . . and how his I.L.A. lieutenants are nearly all criminals." The memo listed the union leader's rumored financial interests in several large shippers (the Anchor Line, Cunard, and United Fruit Company), as well as in stevedoring and trucking firms; and it laid out his network of "police aids and allies," present and former detectives whose protection had long enabled Ryan's "strongarm squads" to intimidate longshoremen on the waterfront.

Johnson also charged that Ryan pocketed all monies from the

yearly honorary dinners of the Joseph P. Ryan Association; that he had once appeared as a character witness for the gangster and racketeer of the Fulton Fish Market Joe "Socks" Lanza. Johnson quoted the DA's report on Ryan's history of surrounding himself with other "gangster associates," from former bootleggers such as Owney Lawlor to the late racketeer George Daggert, to various life-long criminals (Johnny Dunn, Thomas Burke, and Victor Patterson, an "ex-convict with a criminal record dating back to 1915") who'd all become officials in Ryan's union.

Although he'd yet to run down many of the charges himself, Johnson assured his editors that "much of it fits with the picture as obtained on waterfront conditions generally which will be included in the series." If Speed or Bartnett worried over any repercussions from publishing the strong stuff Johnson was gathering, there is no record of their flinching.

CHAPTER 6

THE BIG STORY

One morning in the summer of 1948, the Brooklyn lawyer Jim Longhi found himself at a Chelsea restaurant, nervously settling in across the table from Joe Ryan. It was a command performance with the enemy, since Ryan no doubt remembered Longhi's recent congressional campaign against the Camarda candidate in Red Hook. Still, Ryan had sent word that "he wanted to see me for breakfast, of all things."

Longhi's latest cause was the Brooklyn Back Pay Committee, a collection of waterfront activists and longshoremen demanding lost overtime pay for thousands of hours of dock work owed under the Fair Labor Standards Act. To Joe Ryan, the back pay issue represented one dangerous step toward a regularized workforce on his waterfront, and threatened the existence of the shape-up itself. Ryan had even taken the absurd position of opposing extra pay for his own membership in the name of protecting his union's negotiations from being scrutinized by the courts.

All that summer, as Ryan's men negotiated a modest new contract, the back pay movement gathered force. "We used that back pay issue like a sword against him," Jim Longhi recalled. Eventually, the sword began to cut a little and King Joe asked Longhi to breakfast. The mood was hardly conciliatory. Who could know when he might have another meeting with Ryan, and so the young lawyer laid out the blunt criticisms of Ryan's longshoremen.

Ryan was well known as a hearty old warrior, but Longhi found the president across the table from him spookily disengaged. "The conversation was 'Joe, you know, nothing personal, but you're crazy,'" Longhi remembered. "'How greedy can you get? You know, you are hated.'" As Ryan listened to Longhi, his ruddy face betrayed no doubt in the absolute loyalty of his membership. Finally, he "ducked his head and said, 'The men love me.' That was the end of the conversation."

There wasn't the traditional lull in big news that summer, no absence of vital stories crossing the desks of Keats Speed and Ed Bartnett for passage into their paper. There was the continuing violence in Palestine, where a Jewish state was months away; the Marshall Plan aid to Europe; and the international confrontation with the Soviet Union over the future of a divided Germany; while just blocks from the Sun Building, in the U.S. courthouse in Foley Square, a grand jury had been convened to investigate a possible Soviet espionage ring. At the campaign's outset, the majority of the country's newspaper editors gave President Truman little chance of winning the fall's election. But even in the context of all the newsworthy stories crowding for space that summer, the document the editors received on June 25 was extraordinary. Their general assignment star, who had been poking around the world of the docks since late April, had something fascinating and unwieldy to show for his efforts.

> *Mr. Speed,*
> *Mr. Bartnett:*
> *The attached is a suggested outline for the waterfront crime series which, I hope, will prove as comprehensive as anything the newspapers have ever done on the subject. As you can see, I have a wealth of material, enough, I think, for twenty articles. It is hoped there will be spot news developments on this story once we get rolling . . .*
> *On the BIG STORY back of all this—i.e.: the Syndicate, I can prove no direct link in the waterfront activities, but can state that both State and Federal authorities are convinced such a syndicate exists and that no organized crime in this country can flourish without the knowledge and consent of the Syndicate . . .*
>   *M. Johnson*

Investigative series were still rare in newspapers, let alone series of the size Johnson was proposing: twenty installments covering every facet of the waterfront, from an itemization of its rackets—"systematic thievery, the loading racket, shakedowns, kickbacks, Shylocking, duplicate hiring"—to a piece that would walk the reader around the crime territories that overlay the harbor's familiar shoreline:

> Micky Bowers and his mob control piers from 42nd street up, in Manhattan; Irish gang (Tim O'Meara) in control of the Chelsea district; John Dunn mob in power from 14th street downtown. Italians in control in Brooklyn and on East River piers—members of the old Joe Adonis mob as represented by notorious Al Anastasia.

Lengthy stories asserting a national crime syndicate were difficult to publish in 1948. While spokemen for the Federal Bureau of Narcotics believed solidly in organized crime and a Mafia, J. Edgar Hoover's FBI still held that all gang crime was essentially local. Not only did Johnson outline sections on each of the major gangs as well as on the national syndicate, he also proposed running pictures in the newspaper of the most powerful gangsters (Charlie Luciano, Frank Costello, Meyer Lansky). "The Bowers boys all turn out for the big Joe Ryan testimonial dinners. (We can get pictures of Bowers and mobsters at 1948 dinner)." In addition to telling the reader precisely how each racket functioned, who controlled the gang territories, and how they gained their power, Johnson proposed stories specifically on the syndicate itself. The eighteenth segment was to be a profile called "This Man Costello," while number nineteen promised a fascinating study of "The Underworld Court" told through the experiences of an informer, "Nick," who "tells of getting a hearing before the court at which Trigger Mike Coppola, East Harlem gunman, was on the board of judges. The court's solemn decision and how Nick meekly obeyed it, though he wasn't a member of the syndicate."

Johnson now saw everything in the harbor that Pete Panto had seen. He called organized thievery "the most lucrative of all rackets on the waterfront," totaling perhaps as high as $100 million per year. He would demonstrate the logistics of pilferage through another informer, "who feels he's marked for death, worked with the Bowers gang and gives a play-by-play account of how a large shipment can be stolen from the piers without a trace." The loading racket, waterfront homicides, the Dunn case—each received separate treatment in the four-page outline. A possible clue to his editors that Johnson's series was not already completed and locked in a drawer of his city room desk was the skimpiness of the outline's conclusion, a bland promise to consult law enforcement agencies "as to remedial measures for cleaning up the waterfront . . ."

What Speed and Bart held in their hands promised to bring their paper a lot of attention and a whole lot of trouble. The trouble came first, with threats coming in before the series was even scheduled. Millie Branham remembered the furor that soon started over the waterfront series: "We all called it 'Mike's Soup.' "

CHAPTER 7

THEY'D NEVER KILL A REPORTER

From the high-windowed city room where Mike pounded his Underwood to the commuter village where he lived with his family was only twenty miles. Yet Johnson's nightly train ride seemed to leave him a long way from his waterfront haunts, delivered from the crowded pierheads, waterfront tenements, and dock taverns into squared green yards and avenues named for shade trees and beloved presidents. Johnson had been married to the former Ludie Adams for nearly twenty years, ever since the Georgia couple came north and news of their engagement graced the "Sun's Rays" page in 1928. Now the Johnsons had three children, the elder two in high school, and had recently moved into a fair-size house on Redwood Road in New Hyde Park, just across the boundary where New York City drops away into suburban Long Island. Miss Ludie, who'd trained before marriage to be a classical pianist, had space here for her Steinway, and room out back for a small garden. But as far as their town might feel from Joe Ryan's docks, New Hyde Park was not beyond the city's reach. In this comfortable house in the summer of 1948, the family received the first of a series of frightening phone calls.

Johnson could have brushed off such messages if they came to his desk at the paper, where he often heard from gruff strangers who called him on the sly, some candidates for his growing pool of dock informers. These latest strangers focused instead on calling his home line and terrifying his wife, who was unaccustomed to waterfront talk, let alone death threats. "Sometimes she'd pick up the phone and there'd be these gravelly voiced guys saying, 'You better lay off or else,' " remembered Haynes Johnson, who was then seventeen. "We got a whole series of calls saying, 'We're going to kill you.' It upset my mother terribly." The threats began when Johnson was still hard at work assembling his waterfront material, and the scare campaign escalated in the fall, adding a menace in many voices that became background to the family's routine. During his weeks of investigating, Mike had compiled quite a grim list of stubborn men, both racketeers and reformers like him, who ignored deadly warnings around the harbor. Nevertheless, he assured his family, "They'd never kill a reporter." His son Haynes was never convinced Mike believed it.

The odds of a newsman being murdered by the racketeers may have seemed long, but the investigation Johnson was preparing promised to be unprecedented for its scope and the sheer amount of criminal detail, going beyond the dock rackets to allege a national "syndicate" and name its powerful leaders. The ugly calls his work drew to his house eventually worried Johnson enough that he had the family's home number unlisted. While he continued building the crime series, he confessed another worry to his elder son: "He believed it would never be printed." From across the aisle at rewrite, Millie Falk watched Mike work all summer on his waterfront series and understood his growing fear that it might not see print: "He may have felt they lacked the guts to publish it, that they'd decide that safety was better. It was a bombshell, and the *Sun* hadn't thrown many bombshells."

Whatever Mike thought were his odds of survival that summer, the waterfront mobs demonstrated their own willingness to kill. One of the dock figures he had recently proposed profiling was a New Jersey waterfront gangster known as "Charlie the Jew" Yanowsky. Johnson had researched an entire chapter, to be titled "Alumnus of Alcatraz," on this union-credentialed racketeer he called the Frank Costello of New Jersey. Then, on July 16, after an early dinner at a Hoboken restaurant with two gambler friends, Yanowsky headed off on a long car ride through the Jersey suburbs to keep a mysterious nine o'clock appointment. He was found the next day dumped in a field near a Clifton schoolyard, stabbed a dozen times around his heart with an ice pick. His pockets had been turned out, detectives said, and his wallet was gone, but his diamond ring, his diamond-studded belt buckle, and his card case (containing memberships in the ILA, Marine Warehousemen's, and International Novelty Workers unions) were intact.

Johnson found himself under threat largely because of his grasp of the dock rackets and of the modern criminal phenomenon that Yanowsky personified: the waterfront labor racketeer. Mike had learned that men such as Yanowsky, a machine gunner, hijacker, and narcotics peddler who after prison became a business agent in Joe Ryan's ILA, operated as open secrets on the waterfront. Many had moved into the unions after life in the Prohibition gangs. Like the Camardas across the water in Brooklyn, Yanowsky conducted much of his business through his own local political franchise, as an incorporator of Hoboken's Riverside Democratic Club. Johnson found a gambling house operator who described being the subject of one of Yanowsky's rough business propositions. "Yanowsky said, 'Do I shoot my way in and take it all over, or do I buy my way in for a third interest?' " The gambler quickly welcomed his new partner.

The death of "Charlie the Jew" was a national story, but the headline writer for the *Chicago Tribune* was typical of Mike's press colleagues who were still unsure how to memorialize the powerful Jersey dock boss, as half legitimate or purely underworld:

EX-CONVICT, BUSINESS
AGENT OF 3 UNIONS,
STABBED TO DEATH

Within days of the killing, detectives picked up a well-known union organizer from the West Side docks, Teddy Gleason, at Pier 92, where Mike Johnson had begun his education in the pier rackets that spring. Gleason knew everyone: in addition to his own yearly tribute dinners of the Teddy Gleason Association and his loyal service to the ILA (he wore a diamond ring awarded by Joe Ryan for "untiring efforts at keeping men on the job" during the war), he also crossed paths with gamblers and boxing and Mob men through managing a Jersey hotel where fighters trained. After being picked up by detectives on the waterfront, Gleason was brought to see Johnson's friend in the DA's Homicide Bureau, Bill Keating, who interrogated him about Yanowsky for four hours. The district attorney's office, Johnson wrote in the *Sun*, sought to link the Clifton ice pick murder with pier killings in Manhattan, but investigators got something else.

Keating's demeanor with reporters was uncharacteristically guarded when he emerged from his long, contentious session with Gleason, whom he had placed in the Tombs the previous year as a material witness in another dock murder, the Dunn gang's Manhattan shooting of Anthony Hintz. Despite Keating's unusual reticence that afternoon, Johnson reported that a significant bit of information had emerged: before his death, Yanowsky was "collecting money for an appeal" on behalf of Hintz's convicted killers. This confirmed charges Johnson had repeated in his confidential memo to his editors: that, according to the DA's files, "John Dunn, the gangster now in the death house at Sing Sing . . . is a lieutenant of Ryan's and executes his orders through Teddy Gleason, politician and I.L.A. official . . ."

Charlie Yanowsky had been dead only a couple of weeks when he rose again in the Dunn appeal. The Hintz murder case, argued in court by Bill Keating and George Monaghan the year before, had been a celebrated breakthrough in waterfront prosecutions, and the execution of Cockeye Dunn and company was now set for the end of August 1948. But a new affidavit proposed a dramatically altered account of the murder based on testimony from Andy Sheridan, the poor-sighted gunman whose pistol had so crucially jammed that morning in the Grove Street stairwell, forcing the gang leader, Johnny Dunn, to do all the shooting. Sheridan now claimed to have organized the job, that he had had Hintz killed to defend his own West Side pier holdings, and that his shooter accomplices that morning had been two men who were now conveniently dead or long missing. Their escape car, he added, was supplied by another cohort who'd since passed on, Charlie Yanowsky. Based on this information, the affidavit asked for a new trial for Dunn and Gentile, a two-part ploy that Johnson saw through immediately. Granting the request "would save their lives," he wrote, "and, since he would be needed as a witness, that of Sheridan too, at least through the trial period." Although locked away, Cockeye Dunn was making a clever, dirty fight of it right to the end. All over the waterfront, from Hoboken over to Jane Street and up to Pier 92, Mike saw the connections deepen and multiply.

He kept collecting his dock stories all that summer, typing in his shirtsleeves amid the slowly turning air of the city room, whose windows the staff angled with long-handled poles for relief. "I worked for five months before I ever started writing," Johnson remembered, although he did contribute smaller pieces to the paper, such as the Dunn legal updates, as they emerged from his waterfront work. But at the same time that Johnson was working on his reports, a national political scandal was ready to break out just blocks from the Sun Building. At the U.S. courthouse in Foley Square, a federal grand jury was concluding sixteen months of secret work. Despite the court's proximity, *Sun* hands had only a patchy awareness of the guarded proceedings inside.

What they knew was based largely on the work of their Washington bureau colleague Edward Nellor, who had devoted months to tracking rumors of a federal investigation of Communist espionage groups in the United States. Nellor was young, with slicked dark reddish hair, on the handsome side of baby-faced. He occasionally turned up in the New York office. Ever since the discovery of the Canadian spy ring two years earlier, he had been making himself an expert on the Communist underground in America and was now a virtual clearinghouse for anti-Communist rumors. As even the wispiest spy charges brought embarrassment to the Truman administration, the *Sun*'s conservative publishers gave Nellor wide room to roam. The most spectacular of these half-formed stories—the account of an ex-Communist New York magazine editor whose Maryland farm had served as a drop for a Washington espionage ring in the thirties—would turn out to be true.

Months back, Nellor had reported that the grand jury's details of alleged Communist influence in Washington came from two anonymous sources: a woman party defector and a male editor on a national newsmagazine. In fact, an incredible affidavit detailing the editor's role as a recruiter in a Washington Communist network had passed through Nellor's hands on its way to the FBI. Now, at age thirty-four, Nellor stood ready to open his files to the *Sun*'s readers, as soon as the grand jury's work was concluded. The unidentified editor was Whittaker Chambers.

The federal grand jury had been impaneled the previous summer, in June 1947, its case drawn originally from the recollections of a former Communist messenger whose covert handle was "Clever Girl." The messenger's real name was Elizabeth Bentley, a Vassar graduate in her late thirties from New Milford, Connecticut, who had worked in two wartime "cell" groups that trafficked in information between Washington and Moscow, rendezvousing in ice cream parlors, coffeehouses, and suburban basement darkrooms. Through the travel organization run as a KGB front by her lover, Jacob Golos, she also packed government documents into relief crates for Russia. In 1945, feeling frightened and disillusioned after the death of Golos, Bentley threw herself on the mercy of the FBI and confessed. The Bureau assigned scores of agents to help verify her many claims, and the grand jury case emerged two years later, charging espionage against the federal employees Bentley identified from her former network, which snaked from the Treasury and Commerce departments to the War Production Board. But Bentley, a well-trained courier who had kept little useful evidence of her spy work, lacked outside proof. When it became clear that a grand jury indictment was unlikely without corroboration, federal prosecutors changed their focus, pursuing the easier legal course of charging twelve leaders of the U.S. Communist Party with conspiracy to overthrow the government.

On July 20, Mike Johnson's paper reported that the grand jury's work was finally wrapping up: TOP REDS FACE INDICTMENTS. As Bentley had feared, no one she originally accused was indicted with the dozen Communist Party officials. So she released her story to the New York *World-Telegram*, whose editors, both to conceal her identity and to sell more papers, reimagined the frumpy, dark-haired Bentley as a "svelte blonde," a seductive "mystery woman." The Spy Queen story seized hold of other newspapers, which continued building Bentley up as a glamorous master agent who "vampired information out of government employees," *Time* noted that summer. As the coverage became more torrid, bolder headlines emerged in each afternoon's *Sun*, with fresh testimony from the "woman tipster" trucked out of Reade Street.

Days after the grand jury story broke in late July, congressional subpoenas went out, calling its cast of witnesses down to Washington. The Senate's so-called Ferguson Committee (after its chairman, Homer Ferguson) and the better-known House Committee on Un-American Activities (HUAC) each convened hearings on Communist infiltration of the government. But this midsummer Washington drama had not been on the government schedule. The congressmen were in town only because Harry Truman had ended their vacations. Twelve hours after securing the renomination of his party for the presidency, Truman called back what he termed the "second worst congress in history" from its summer recess and into emergency session, hoping to force votes on stalled but urgent legislation, including his own anti-inflation measures. But if he had been vexed by the combative Eightieth Congress before he cut short their break, he was further angered by the leadership's response: HUAC, overcoming its low reputation after the previous year's rancorous investigation of communism in the movie industry, now found new life in the hunt for subversives in the federal government.

On July 30, the Spy Queen made her first Washington appearance, testifying before the Senate's Ferguson Committee for five hours. If she didn't measure up to the physical image that newsmen had dreamed for her, the world she evoked of life as a KGB courier was certainly exotic. (*The New Yorker*'s A. J. Liebling reflected the disappointment of many once the dowdy truth of the Spy Queen was revealed, calling the Connecticut-born Bentley a "Nutmeg Mata Hari.") As a witness, she had authenticity, if little proof.

Bentley had left no useful paper trail of her exploits, but Whittaker Chambers, the long-rumored "New York magazine editor," had kept decade-old evidence stashed with paranoid precision all around his Maryland farm (the drop site Edward Nellor had reported on in October 1947). Days after Bentley's initial testimony, Chambers appeared before the House committee, a soft-spoken, portly, somewhat fatalistic character in a banker's suit. Bentley had clearly enjoyed recounting her adventures in the underground, but Chambers seemed to be grimly performing a duty. He "read his statement in quiet, shaken tones," wrote Nellor, "but the substance of his remarks was loaded with political and security T.N.T." Like Bentley, Chambers darkly sketched out a network devoted to "the Communist infiltration of the American government." Then he named Alger Hiss, a former State Department official who was now the head of the Carnegie Endowment for World Peace, as one of its agents. As Hiss and other accused conspirators appeared in Washington to defend themselves, an emerging political scandal found its legs. When President Truman called the proceedings a sideshow hunt for "red herrings," the battle was joined and the fall election, in which Truman already trailed New York's Republican governor, Thomas Dewey, was in high gear.

CHAPTER 8

THE LEECH AND THE THUG

The hearings' themes of loyalty and subversion were echoed that August back in New York, where the state convention of the American Federation of Labor took over the Hotel Commodore. Joe Ryan introduced an amendment to the AFL's state charter, denying a seat to any potential delegate who refused to "affirm to the satisfaction of the credentials committee that they are not Communists or members of any other party seeking to overthrow by force the Government of the United States . . ." Over his two decades as the longshore union president, Ryan had forcefully wielded the charge of communism against his enemies of all persuasions, whether actually Red or merely defiant. He had thrown it successfully at the organizers of the portwide rebellion against his leadership three years before, and since the war, his men had refused to handle the cargoes of Eastern Bloc vessels. When a Yugoslav liner arrived in port that summer bearing state portraits of Stalin and Tito in its lounge, passengers lugged their own baggage and the ship's crew did its best, working the winches into the night.

Ryan had been fighting the cold war on the waterfront since long before he knew a name for it, especially against his rival, the Australian radical leader of the West Coast longshore union, Harry Bridges. While not registered as a Communist, the militant Bridges acted in harmony with the Party's line and, over the years of their feud, had vowed publicly to expand his movement east into Ryan's ports.

For Ryan, the Hotel Commodore's Grand Ballroom had a kind of home field intimacy. Over the years of his presidency it had been the site of many of his own testimonial dinner-dances, when senators, mayors, and governors (one a future U.S. president) toasted him before well-dressed crowds of gamblers, bootleggers, Tammany pols, and waterfront powers named Dunn, Bowers, Mangano, or Anastasia. This was the ballroom stage where Governor Franklin Roosevelt had served as honorary chairman on a gala night long ago, and where the former New York City mayor Jimmy Walker saluted Ryan alongside the powerful boss of Jersey City, Frank Hague. On a spring night in 1938 the great reformer Fiorello La Guardia grumpily attended, along with his police commissioner; their table setting was courtesy of an arrangements committee that included "Cockeye" Dunn. Other years' gatherings brought out all five borough presidents in their tuxes, or drew the great lightweight fighter Benny Leonard with the heavyweight champion himself, James J. Braddock, who was really an old Jersey longshoreman anyway. And this past spring, the Jersey docks boss Charlie Yanowsky had crossed the river to be seen at table number 115, weeks before he was murdered. (The annual Joseph P. Ryan Association dinner generated "a substantial sum realized in sale of tickets, souvenir programs and advertising space therein," Mike Johnson informed the city desk. "This money goes to Ryan.")

Whatever strains were lately showing in King Joe's union, the drawing (and earning) power of the Ryan dinner remained undimmed.

Now a less-harmonious scene met Ryan's eye as he scanned the Hotel Commodore's Grand Ballroom, where, as requested, the AFL's Credentials Committee had denied seats to twenty-seven delegates on suspicion of Communist activity. When the president of a Meat Cutters local appealed from the floor that the barred delegates be heard by the full convention, he was shouted down and Joe Ryan's amendment was adopted, 1,094 votes to 5. That done, Ryan returned to the business of the harbor, where his union faced ongoing investigations by the DA's office and the *Sun*, and where a growing dissonance among its membership threatened the latest contract, with the old one due to expire on August 21. In addition to rebel longshoremen pushing for a strike and a shipping association bracing hard for it, Ryan now had to worry about federal mediators in his port, sent by a nervous President Truman.

The last time Joe Ryan had met a serious threat from his own membership was in 1945, when, though still daubed with dark brownout paint, the city was restlessly emerging from the years of wartime controls. While the waterfront's basic balance of power remained as before, the combat experiences of many returning dockers had left them less fearful of the racketeers. That October, angered over their proposed contract, some thirty-five thousand longshoremen launched a wildcat strike to unseat their "lifetime president." "On New York's waterfront, kingdom of the leech and the thug," wrote Maurice Rosenblatt in *The Nation*, "they were rebelling against Joseph P. Ryan . . . charged with being the kingpin of a dictatorship which uses terror to exploit the men." After dragging on for eighteen days, the attempted coup failed, and Ryan proclaimed the end of the uprising another victory over communism. (One of the men's chief concerns—the dangerous wartime trebling in the size of cargo slingloads—was left unaddressed in the settlement, but the daily shape-ups were reduced from three to two.) As for the strike's leaders, two were beaten up and expelled from the union. Mike Johnson cited the explanation of the labor authority Reverend Benjamin Masse: "Asked whether [William] Warren might return to work, an ILA delegate winked and said, 'Sure, he can report, but if he falls and hurts himself, it'll be no one's fault.' The day after the strike ended, Warren reported to work—and fell and hurt himself, i.e., he was beaten up. Nice place, the New York waterfront."

Anyone who spent much time around the docks in the summer of 1948 knew that another portwide strike was a growing possibility. With the contract deadline of August 21 only days away, Ryan announced that an insurgent group was stirring up his longshoremen with dangerous leaflets accusing him of betraying the membership and acting as a front man for the shippers. These agitators, he told reporters, were "part of a world-wide Communist plan to create trouble on the waterfront."

Whether or not a strike had Joe Ryan's blessing, Harry Truman could not wait and run the risk of forty-five thousand longshoremen tying up the nation's ports. He did have a new weapon at his disposal, the Labor-Management Relations (or Taft-Hartley) Act, designed by the Republican Congress Truman had recently disparaged and ordered back into summer session. The law, which Truman had tried to veto as anti-labor, was created in 1947 in the wake of the national labor uprising that came with the end of the war. Under Taft-Hartley, a president could order a "cooling-off" period of several months if a contract dispute threatened "national health and safety" in vital industries.

On the day before the August strike deadline, on the recommendation of his fact-finding board, Truman instructed Attorney General Tom Clark to seek an injunction under the Taft-Hartley provisions. "[In] my opinion," Truman wrote, "these disputes threaten to result in strikes or lockouts affecting a substantial part of the maritime industry [which] will imperil the national health and safety." The request reached the desk of federal judge Harold Medina the same week he ruled against the twelve Communist Party officials seeking more time to respond to the grand jury's conspiracy charges handed up in July. When Medina granted Truman's petition for an injunction, it made any job action by the Atlantic Coast longshoremen illegal for eighty days and delayed the port showdown to November 9, safely on the far side of the presidential election.

"If there is a strike, the public should ascertain whether it has been sanctioned or not," Joe Ryan warned, sounding strangely meek. Judge Medina was more hopeful about the possibilities for negotiations under the injunction, remarking that the two sides in the longshore dispute seemed "reasonable" to him. But as Mike Johnson had already discovered, hearing the bitter pledges around the harbor, reasonable times were not in store. The big strike was coming, if it had to roll over King Joe himself.

September arrived with all sides in the port dispute cooling under federal order, even as Ryan's Pacific Coast nemesis, Harry Bridges, led his own longshoremen in closing piers from Portland to San Diego in a distant contract struggle that Ryan followed like angry weather.

CHAPTER 9

A LOUSY BUCK

By September, Johnson was finally writing his crime series "in earnest."

What he had first seen as just a "ripping good crime story"— the murder of a hiring boss by racketeers—had deepened under the weight of testimonies from his hard-won collection of witnesses and defectors. The death of Thomas Collentine had led him from the Upper Manhattan neighborhood where Collentine was shot in the street to the dicey West Side headquarters of the Bowers gang who'd likely killed him. From there, the trail branched into the union that shielded the racketeers. And so Johnson worked his way down the Manhattan shoreline, digging into the seemingly legit and the notorious, and everything between. "I worked for about five months, investigating, assimilating and sifting material before I ever started writing," he remembered. "I haunted waterfront saloons, met criminal 'stool pigeons' in their hideaways, attended union meetings, questioned murder witnesses, studied the union's consti-

tution, scanned the police records of dozens of waterfront gangsters, and interviewed hundreds of dock workers."

Informants had come compliments of the *Sun*'s courts reporter,
Morty Davis, or referred by an old friend in the FBI, Ed Conroy, or
thanks to Bill Keating's sneaky generosity with the DA's files. To
understand how the money side worked, Johnson questioned a former Mob accountant, "Charlie M," in addition to his skittish onetime Bowers functionary, "Joe"; Buster Smith, surprisingly helpful
after two shootings by the Dunn gang; and "Nick," who'd experi-
enced rare mercy from a syndicate "court."

As Labor Day approached, the big concern around the city room
was no longer the potential strike by East Coast longshoremen, nor
was there terrific excitement over the coming presidential election,
which already seemed lopsidedly uninteresting as Harry Truman
and Thomas Dewey prepared to set out on railroad campaign tours.
There was now an inevitability to Dewey, the Republican challenger. As he crossed the country in his long Victory Special in
early September, he led Truman by eleven points, causing one
bored national pollster to pronounce Dewey's election a "foregone
conclusion."

For those who weren't crowding the roads out of New York for
the Labor Day weekend, the nervous focus—beyond the daily
threats between Russia and the Western powers over delivery of the
Marshall aid to Berlin—was on yet another in the national rash of
strikes. At the same time as the holiday exodus from the city, striking teamsters at the Holland Tunnel were turning back other freight
haulers entering New York. The local walkout by ten thousand
wholesale truckers cut off hundreds of deliveries—stranding loads
of groceries, liquor shipments, fall fashions from the Garment District, even rolls of newsprint, which launched a race at dailies such
as the *Sun* between the duration of the strike and dwindling in-
house stores of paper. A minister at St. Stephen's Episcopal Church

in Manhattan called the truckers' action "a wet blanket dampening public enthusiasm for this year's observance of Labor Day." Many of that weekend's sermons on the unions were loftily forgettable, but the address planned by a young Jesuit priest from the West Side promised to be powerfully different.

As he typed up the provocative opening sections of his crime series, Mike Johnson was unaware that another critic of Ryan and the racketeers was about to declare himself. Father John Corridan, S.J., a tall, large-eyed, balding Irishman in his late thirties, did not immediately present—in his black suit and dog collar around his long neck—the figure of the hard-smoking and sometimes profane man known by colleagues. He had begun appearing around the Chelsea docks the year before, a darkly sober character shadowing the morning shape-up, glaring at any stevedore whose hiring style seemed tainted. Like Mike Johnson, he maintained a personal library of waterfront vice, numbered files on "crime & racketeering" stuffed with clippings and court testimonies about public loading, dope smuggling, gunrunning, bookmaking, loan-sharking, and notable pilferages of jewelry, lumber, coffee, cases of Scotch, or even large machinery—not to mention collected scraps of unflattering trivia on dock bosses and shipping executives. While the Father and the reporter had been crossing much the same ground on their separate crusades, it wasn't until that fall of 1948 that Mike finally met the "waterfront priest."

As he crossed the harbor to Jersey City, Father Corridan was armed to give the speech of his life. The audience he had chosen for his Labor Day talk was a roomful of Catholic laymen gathered at the Paulus Hook Council of the Knights of Columbus, all curious to learn about his experiences as a priest along the West Side docks, and all sharing his contempt for the Communists' message. After his posting at the Xavier Institute of Industrial Relations in 1946, Corridan's longshoremen students had educated him with brutal

tales of the waterfront rackets and the shape-up, "a system calcu-
lated to produce the most bucks" for everyone, he learned, except
for the men who submitted to it. He'd heard about the life of Pete
Panto and other rebels from his first friends on the docks, a group
of twenty longshoremen who enrolled in the labor school to challenge the Dunn-McGrath mob over hiring on nearby piers. Waterfront hands such as Christy Doran and Arthur "Brownie" Browne
became Father Corridan's initial guides to the rougher parts of
"dockland." What the young priest learned stoked his anger, and
gradually pushed him beyond his sympathetic role and into open
advocacy. With his Labor Day address, "Christ Looks at the Waterfront," Father Corridan planned to go public with his outrage.

The Knights of Columbus was a fitting venue for Corridan to test
his message. Either the Knights crowd would follow the ambitious
conceit of his talk—imagining Jesus Christ touring the money
fields of the racketeers and even shaping up for work beside the
men—or there would be puzzled, polite silence as they waited for
Father to wind it up. He surprised some in the room the moment he
opened his mouth and began sermonizing in his streetwise New
York accent: "You want to know what's wrong with the waterfront?
It's love of a lousy buck, whether it's one or a thousand or ten thousand . . . God or no God, a man is going to get them in any way he
can. In many ways, you can't blame the Mob."

Behind the collar was a neighborhood tough guy bearing earthy
witness to a world that sounded pretty far from standard pulpit fare.
Father Corridan had grown up mostly on the West Side, in the kind
of tough parish where "half the kids raised in parochial schools
grow up to be mobsters," he told a reporter. "The other half become
priests. It's so tough that it seems you have to go to one extreme or
the other. There's no middle ground." As the eldest son of an
"incorruptible" Irish patrolman, Corridan resisted the pull of Mob
life, but didn't feel drawn to the other extreme until later.

Like Joe Ryan and Mike Johnson, Corridan had lost his father while he was still a boy. His mother, Hannah Corridan, raised her five sons on a police widow's pension, adding boarders to their crowded home and doing domestic work. After high school, Corridan reached Wall Street as an office boy in a securities house; he had advanced to handling sales transactions when, at twenty, he opened the book that would upend and redirect his life: René Fülöp-Miller's *The Power and Secret of the Jesuits.* He entered seminary, where his attempts to curb his swearing earned him the nickname Pete within the order, blurting "For Pete's sake" instead of "some of the more lurid phrases from the classic doric of the gutter," wrote his friend Father Philip Carey, director of the Xavier labor school.

The school sat just off Fifth Avenue, on Sixteenth Street, in the basement of Xavier's five-story gray-granite building. What began as the Xavier Institute of Social Studies later had its mission redefined in the spirit of the 1930s Catholic Social Action movement, educating union people against the blare of atheistic communism. As Father Carey told the writer Jules Weinberg in 1948, "Neither communists nor racketeers can stand democracy." The waterfront had both kinds, Father Corridan heard from those longshoremen brave enough to enroll in the school's self-defense workshops in negotiations, labor economics, or the basics of running a clean union meeting. (When the *Harper's* writer Mary Heaton Vorse visited Corridan, his office more resembled a detectives' squad room as she overheard him correcting two friends: " 'No, no. Johnny Cockeye never used the concrete. He used what is called the Chinese Method entirely—a quick bullet in the back of the head and the car radio turned up.")

As he spoke to the Knights on Labor Day, Father Corridan had anticipated one reaction to his unorthodox talk: "I suppose some people would smirk at the thought of Christ in the shape. It is about as absurd as the fact that He carried carpenter's tools in His hands and earned his bread and butter by the sweat of his brow. As absurd as the fact that Christ redeemed all men irrespective of their race, color, or station in life."

Corridan next pictured Christ like the dockworkers he knew: burdened by "bread and butter and meat bills and rent" as they joined the morning cattle call. Jesus "stands in the shape knowing that all won't get work and maybe He won't," Corridan boomed. He "works on a certain pier. He knows that He is expected to be deaf, dumb, and blind, if He wants to work. Some people think that the Crucifixion only took place on Calvary."

The priest from the waterfront walked his audience through the dockers' world, as Christ sat in on a sham union meeting where the officers all flashed their diamond rings and collected booty "from 14th and 8th" (Ryan's offices). He noticed the glut of neighborhood saloons tempting men near the piers, and heard from tenement wives fighting to keep the family wages away from bartenders.

"Christ works on a pier and His back aches because there are a fair number of the 'boys' on the pier. They don't work, but they have their rackets at which so many wink."

At the end of his pitiful tour, Father Corridan warned:

For those longshoremen who are straight and are good family men, God be praised.

For those who slip every once in a while and lose hope, God have mercy. To those responsible, God grant the grace to see things on the waterfront as Christ sees them, for the time is growing short when God will show no mercy.

Everything in the priest's later career was laid out in this fiercely simple chastening of the dockers and their bosses, what would become a stump speech in his growing campaign against the racketeers. When he gathered up his pages that day and returned to his basement office across the harbor, Father Corridan knew he had declared a kind of war.

Early on the Saturday after Labor Day, during the hours when hundreds of finches and warblers unaccountably flew straight into the upper lighted windows of the Empire State Building before kite-tailing to the pavement, New York's week-old truckers' strike began to fold up. Like Christ in his Labor Day speech, Corridan soon returned to his tours of the West Side waterfront, noting names and casting a cold eye on the gangsters' agents, most of them fellow Catholics he hoped to shame. "You've got to remember the kind of thing you are fighting," he would tell Mike Johnson. "It's a fight with no holds barred, and sometimes you've got to knee and gouge and elbow in the clinches. I do what I have to do." That fall of 1948, the Xavier labor school was celebrating the recent victory led by two of its students, who'd maneuvered the head of their own Transport Workers Union, "Red" Mike Quill, into seeking a raise in the popular nickel fare, against the wishes of his backers in the Communist Party. Now, with one of their own having openly sided with the anti-Ryan forces, the school's leaders braced for an expanded feud with Ryan and the gangsters.

CHAPTER 10

A CUP OF COFFEE

Andy Sheridan left his death row cell at Sing Sing dressed in one of his sharp civilian suits for the pastoral ride into the city. He was making this supervised October visit to Manhattan because of what he'd said to a priest at the prison the August before. His prison confession had evolved into an affidavit for a new trial for his two codefendants in the murder of boss stevedore Anthony "Andy" Hintz, left gut-shot but temporarily alive in the stairwell of his West Village apartment house in January 1947. The petition eventually brought Sheridan to this General Sessions hearing in Manhattan, facing the same judge who'd presided over his murder case. With its details about pier rackets and gangster rivalries, Sheridan's new hearing promised to be a dark preview of the criminal story Mike Johnson had spent months uncovering. "The union—it was just a front for the rackets," explained Sheridan, who had dabbled in both between gang executions.

To many in the courtroom that first Wednesday in October,

Squint Sheridan's confession seemed less a product of his rebellious conscience than of the offstage manipulations of his old boss, Johnny Dunn, who was also facing electrocution. After the Court of Appeals and Supreme Court had each passed on Dunn's prior legal queries, Sheridan made his prison confession absolving Dunn and Gentile. "I knew I was going to the chair in a short time and that nothing could save me," Sheridan explained under oath about his change of heart. "I figured it was the only decent thing to do. I was trying to help out two fellows who had nothing to do with this case. And that's the God's truth."

As the hearing began, Johnson watched the large, soft-faced convict settle into the witness box, his "blue eyes gleaming behind thick glasses" as he told how he'd planned the murder for which he'd been sent to the death house. In his new telling, Sheridan claimed that the real shooters were two other hoodlums named Jeff Lepore and John Duff. One was confirmed dead from a railway accident; the other had been suspiciously lost for the past twenty-one months. "Sheridan implicated still another man, now dead, in the murder plot—Charles Yanowsky," noted Johnson. It had been Yanowsky who "supplied the stolen automobile used by the killers in making their getaway . . ." Under pressure of a fierce and lengthy cross-examination, Sheridan also laid the fatal guns at Charlie's door, clearing the actual supplier, Dunn's gangster brother-in-law, Ed McGrath, who remained vividly alive.

Sheridan now insisted that the murder had not originated with Dunn's desire to control hiring privileges at Hintz's Jane Street pier, but was a consequence of Sheridan's own deadly rivalry with Hintz over loading fees and control of an ILA local. "Hintz was out to kill me and I was out to kill him," said Sheridan. After passing out the guns and warning his men not to stay out drinking the night before, "I instructed Lepore to empty his gun at Hintz and put all the shot in his head." On the morning of the murder, Sheridan was not standing in Hintz's stairwell cursing his own jammed gun, he claimed, but was waiting by the phone in a Jersey City hotel room for word that Hintz had been professionally "clipped." Mike Johnson wrote that Sheridan "repeated over and over again that he was not sorry he had engineered the murder of Hintz. Planning the killing was 'just like ordering a cup of coffee,' he agreed at one point. It gave him no trouble at all." It was the "cup of coffee" line that most reporters seized on in summing up the gangster's sweaty few hours on the stand. "Taking human life meant nothing to you?" the prosecutor asked. "Not Andy Hintz's life," Sheridan answered. "He was no bargain."

Bargain or not, the dead man himself was soon heard from, in sworn testimony that Dunn's lawyers had successfully blocked at the original trial. Before Hintz's death in the hospital, Cockeye Dunn had been summoned to the victim's room for a dramatic bedside identification. As Dunn stood nearby, Hintz said firmly, "That's the man who shot me." Then, enraged at having his killer patronize him and ask if he was "rational," Hintz plucked at his hospital pajamas, trying to show Dunn his wounds. "Show him where I got it," he said to Bill Keating, who would lead Dunn's prosecution. "Show him to see if he is satisfied."

Clearly a lot of work had gone into Squint Sheridan's affidavit and courtroom performance, but it was all quickly swept aside by the words of the murder victim. On October 19, Judge McClellan refused the application for a new trial, calling the whole legal exercise "the well-known trick of the underworld of substituting for guilty participants dead men whose lips are sealed." Dunn, Gentile, and Sheridan were now scheduled to die the week of November 15. As he had always done before, Cockeye Dunn would have to find another route to save himself.

Mike Johnson was known to keep books by William Faulkner or Dashiell Hammett in his desk, and would urge good ones on colleagues around the city room. Like Hammett's Continental Op in *Red Harvest*, bluffing his way through the corrupt layers of the town of Poisonville to arrive at the office of its amiably crooked police chief, he had spent months picking his way along the piers to reach the door of Joe Ryan, the public face of the working harbor, who at last consented to an interview that fall. Here Johnson finally was in Ryan's sunny office high above the Chelsea rooftops. A window sat off either padded shoulder of the man reclining heavily before him in a studded leather chair. When Johnson looked slightly left or right as they talked, he could pick out distant harbor scenes through the dusty glass—a silvered bit of river ruffled by barge traffic between Chelsea and Hoboken, a sling of crates rising from behind the elevated highway, freshly dumped rail freight crossing from Weehawken, a tug returning from showing a liner to its West Side berth.

In his double-breasted suit, the ruddy-faced man at the president's desk was broader than in the romantic wall portrait of himself as a young turk, his forehead fringed then by dark, tousled hair as if he'd taken a justified swing before assuming his pose. Now, with his gray hair parted and slicked down, Joe Ryan braced for what was in his visitor's notebook: no doubt a familiar litany about goon squads and kickbacks and other slanders gathered from old Rackets Bureau reports, dropped murder cases, and the flimsy fictions of jailhouse snitches.

Though Johnson's questions were tough, he put them across rather softly, in a respectful, vaguely southern voice. But underneath these surface manners, Ryan easily gathered his visitor's low opinion of the union to which he'd lent his life. Joe finally answered by thumping the glass top of his dark-wood desk.

"That's ridiculous!" he roared, puffing up with practiced indignation as Johnson scribbled. "Where is the Police Department? We got a Police Department, haven't we? The police wouldn't stand for a situation like that. Our men wouldn't stand for it. The steamship and stevedoring companies wouldn't stand for it."

Johnson was finally seeing the personality up close as Ryan blustered through the conversational hazards: "The kickback? I defy anybody to prove there's any kickback in our organization. I don't care who says so, and they have been saying it for years. It's never been proved."

The enmity between Johnson and Ryan was inevitable for reasons of both substance and political style. Not only was the newsman crusading all over the boss's docks, but their mutual dislike was also based in a surprising similarity: both were strong union men. Unlike the owner of the paper that allowed him to hold forth about "labor gangsterism," Johnson was a dues-paying believer in the union ideal. As a young reporter, he had been present at the founding of the Newspaper Guild, created amid many highballs and speeches over a series of evenings in Heywood Broun's apartment in 1933. The labor "organization" in which Ryan now wrapped himself offended Johnson as a thuggish cartoon of unionism.

During his own brief, bewildering meal with Ryan, the labor lawyer Jim Longhi had discovered how Joe could control an encounter even when he seemed to have none of the ammunition. When Johnson now asked him about the numbers of ex-convicts who moved so easily from prison into ILA jobs, Ryan answered, "We welcome ex-convicts—well, maybe welcome is too broad a statement . . . But we believe every man, regardless of what he has done, has a right to a second chance. . . . There are some criminals on the waterfront, but they are in the minority and don't run in packs. Ninety-nine percent of the men in our organization are decent, hardworking, God-fearing men. Men with families, trying to make a living."

Johnson waved more dirty names—of the gangsters and even murderers who'd found their way into the union as officers, including Andy Sheridan's late friend Charlie Yanowsky, the Jersey racketeer and secretary in a warehouse local whose name echoed through so many underworld stories. Ryan hardly blinked explaining the elevation of Yanowsky, a bare acquaintance who had attended Ryan's testimonial dinner: "I didn't want him. The first time I saw him, right here in this office, I said he couldn't have the job. He said the men wanted him and had elected him and what was I going to do about it? And what could I do? I'll say this for Yanowsky: he done a good job."

Johnson was not the first reporter to observe how Ryan was both king and captive. Although President Ryan's hands had been mysteriously tied in the Yanowsky matter, Charlie had nevertheless "done a good job" before he was ice-picked the previous July.

His notebook was quickly filling with Ryan's evasions, but Johnson pushed on: What about the loading racket? "Why, every district attorney for years back has investigated the loading racket—I mean the so-called loading racket—and hasn't found anything." The shape-up? "The men have never asked for a change. . . . There must be some reason, some benefit from the shape-up, or they'd change it."

At last either Johnson had worn through Ryan's patience or Joe had hammered through the reporter's questions, and the session ran out. "I'll stand back of everything I've said," Ryan assured his visitor. "Let 'em prove all this stuff you have been hearing about." Johnson pocketed his notes and left the sunlit skirmishing of the president's office for the elevator ride down to the lobby. He reached the Eighth Avenue sidewalk certain he'd had an audience with a dictator.

CHAPTER 11

MEET THE BOYS

Johnson had a lot on his mind when he entered the voting booth and loyally pulled the lever for the Democrat, Harry Truman. His bad luck in Saturday-night poker games had enriched his colleagues over the years, and yet in recent days he had spread a number of long-shot bets around the office on the remote chance of a Truman win. As he rode from New Hyde Park into the city on Election Day, he was dreading the prospect of paying off if Tom Dewey prevailed as expected. But the big vote wasn't all that weighed on his mind that morning. Johnson's crime series was finally slated to start the following Monday, the day before the anti-strike injunction ended in the longshoremen's fight. With the election out of the way, Johnson's waterfront account could claim the front page, revealing what the *Sun* billed as "A Cesspool of Crime."

Johnson's friends in the city room were not alone in predicting Dewey's election. Most of the country's best-known political writers were preparing to put to bed a presidential campaign that had rarely seemed competitive. "The problem is not how to beat Truman," Walter Lippmann declared over the summer, "but how to preserve the victory beyond 1948." In Southern California one day in late September, the two candidates' trains had crossed paths, Truman's whistlestopping its way from Los Angeles and into the Democratic South, and Dewey's Victory Special bearing him to a mass rally at the Hollywood Bowl, where, swept by movie premiere lights, he demanded a "war of truth" against Soviet propaganda. However closely their campaign tours passed that afternoon, the two men never crossed in the polls, which held steadily for Dewey until he checked into his rooms at New York's Roosevelt Hotel on Election Day, to await word of his victory. The *Sun* had Dewey poised to claim thirty-two states, while the governor was pictured as "The Next President" inside the November *Life. Newsweek* projected a win by four million votes, and *Kiplinger's* devoted its entire issue to "What Dewey Will Do." The Times Square crowd that gathered to follow the expected rout that night was understandably lighter than for past elections. By the time Truman went to bed early in Missouri, even his wife, Bess, had urged him to make peace with his inevitable drubbing.

Having predicted a Republican "sweep," the New York *Sun* was hardly the only paper in the country to go deep into election night ready with an eight-column headline declaring Tom Dewey the new president. Three fourths of the country's daily newspapers had favored Dewey, but by the *Sun*'s deadline hour, the votes from generally Republican western states had not yet overcome Truman's early lead from East Coast cities. "I was on the lobster shift as a copyboy on election night," recalled Les Woodcock, then a twenty-year-old student who discreetly backed Truman. "As the returns came in over the AP wire that Truman was making a strong showing, the mood in the city room slowly turned sour. I can't remember when it became apparent that Dewey had lost during that long night, but I do remember George Van Slyke, the editorial writer, staring gloomily into space from his desk in a corner overlooking Broadway. We were kept busy running copy as the returns came in, but it was fairly quiet in the city room when I left."

The great Baltimore columnist and contrarian H. L. Mencken had spent more than four decades in newspapers and followed eleven presidential races before casting the final vote of his life, reluctantly for Dewey. That summer of 1948 he poured scorn over the Democrats and Republicans, each holding conventions in the Philadelphia heat; he considered the appeals to southern pride of Strom Thurmond's Dixiecrats, who had bolted from Truman's convention over a proposed civil rights platform; and he suffered through the pieties of Henry Wallace's Progressives meeting at night in Philadelphia's Shibe Park ("Just as the magic name was pronounced the candidate himself appeared athwart the home-plate in a shiny open car"). Over the long political season, Mencken heard only one address he could unguardedly admire: a rhetorical beauty by the Princeton-educated Socialist candidate Norman Thomas, then making his sixth consecutive run for president, given to a small gathering above a Chinese restaurant. Mencken considered Dewey's stump speeches blandly statesman-like by comparison, even if their sentences were well formed and sonorously spoken. As for the president, Mencken tapped out an election night column calling Truman a "third-rate rabble-rouser" allied with the "labor racketeers."

As the Dewey victory stalled hour after hour, the press section where Mencken waited became increasingly tense and smoky. "Sitting among my colleagues," he wrote, "as the returns began to come in, I felt and shared the tremors and tickles that ran up and down their vertebrae. How could so many wizards be so thumpingly wrong?" The wizards had gambled that Truman would be punished by the defections of Wallace's Progressives and Thurmond's Dixiecrats; instead, the president held on to win 28 states and 303 electoral votes, beating Dewey by 2 million. On November 3, the New York *Sun* acknowledged the emerging upset: ELECTION IN DOUBT.

That morning after the vote, Mike Johnson happily made his rounds at the paper to gather up his bet money. At 11:15, Governor Dewey conceded the inconceivable, and by early afternoon he stood before a group of 150 humbled reporters, whom he assured, "I'm just as surprised as you are and I gather that that surprise is shared by everybody." When one newsman asked for Dewey's thoughts on the pollsters who'd spent the fall touting his coming triumph, he answered, "I hate to comment on anyone else's misfortune." Tom Dewey then left the last press conference of his candidacy for a long, subdued ride back to Albany. Writers immediately blamed their fallen favorite for everything from his Gable-ish mustache to his overconfident campaign. In the early hours of November 4, when the president's *Ferdinand Magellan* stopped in St. Louis long enough for Harry Truman to step onto the rear of the train and meet reporters, one of them passed him the election edition of the *Chicago Daily Tribune*. Flashbulbs popped in the dark and cameras caught his grin as he held up the defiant front page: DEWEY DEFEATS TRUMAN.

While news of Truman's upset win crossed the country, a Jesuit priest from New York was making his own arrangements to travel to Washington, but not to join the celebrations. The president was still riding home to the capital on November 4 when John Corridan and a colleague from the Xavier labor school, Bernard Fitzpatrick, boarded an early morning train out of Pennsylvania Station. Corridan wanted to warn the president's people about the possibility of a paralyzing strike by East Coast longshoremen. The Chelsea priest who had openly declared himself with the dockers in a Labor Day speech in Jersey City was now making himself their champion with the administration. It was Fitzpatrick who'd had the connections to get a hearing with the labor adviser and assistant to the president John Steelman, but the travelers' roles were clear: Fitzpatrick had secured the meeting, but Corridan would deliver the sermon. Over breakfast in the dining car, rolling through the marshes, farms, factory towns, and port cities on their way to Washington, the two men plotted out what to tell Truman's experts to do about the embattled waterfront.

They arrived in Washington before lunch. The election had just pulled everyone giddily back from the brink of unemployment, and Corridan sensed an " 'out of the valley of death' elation" in the White House corridors. Once they were settled in John Steelman's office, the tall, balding priest spoke urgently about harbor rackets and union gangsterism, bringing a note of outside gravity to the meeting. After hearing his visitors out, Steelman remarked, "Gentlemen, you are not leaving this hot potato in my lap," and arranged to pass the New Yorkers on to his friend Cyrus Ching, head of the Federal Mediation and Conciliation Service, later that afternoon.

Since its creation the year before under the Taft-Hartley Act, the FMCS was where labor crises of any real magnitude converged. Its head, Cy Ching, was the right man for a strike-heavy age: a confident, well-mannered, cerebral mediator who believed in the defusing power of talk and did not suffer grandstanding. Assured but not partisan, he was a Canadian-born Republican serving at the pleasure of a Democratic American president. Cartoonists loved contrasting Ching's elongated, gentlemanly figure with a gathering labor storm. He was seventy-two years old and had already retired from his civilian career—first at Boston's West End Street Railway and later as director of labor relations at U.S. Rubber—before his reputation for edging disputants toward common ground made him the government's head mediator. Ching, who traditionally voted Republican, nevertheless had made some side money that autumn by betting on his boss with a colleague who gave twenty-to-one odds that Dewey would win. "I took a nice bite out of him," Ching remembered.

Ching leaned his six-foot-seven-inch body back in his swivel chair and puffed at his clay-bowl pipe as his visitors from New York described the feudal-sounding network of "fiefdoms" rimming the harbor. He already had people dispatched to mediate the weeks-old dock strike on the West Coast led by Joe Ryan's hated union rival, "The Nose," Harry Bridges. How bad, Ching wanted to know, were things in the east by comparison? Corridan warned that "any temporary solution" of the crisis would not address the "evil condition" of the port's basic labor system. Corridan showed Ching the dramatic accident figures for longshoremen, and pointed out how the shape-up hiring method inspired graft through its permanent glut of workers, and made it more difficult to screen out potential saboteurs. Given the tenor of the men, a revolt against their own union leadership was inevitable. "I had spoken the burning truth as I knew it," Father Corridan told his biographer.

After thanking Ching for his time, Corridan and Fitzpatrick headed back to Union Station a day ahead of the presidential train that would deliver Harry Truman, his route lined by more than seven hundred thousand people and contrite banners like the one stretched across the *Washington Post*'s second floor: WELCOME HOME FROM CROW-EATERS.

Back on the West Side, Father Corridan learned that ILA members voting in a federal ballot had rejected the shippers' most recent offer by ten to one. Given that Ryan's negotiating committee had just recommended this same deal, Corridan sensed a rebellion in the making. He proposed a quick article to the labor editor at the Jesuit journal *America*, explaining the reasons behind the coming walkout. Corridan planned to run off ten thousand copies of his remarks and distribute them up and down the waterfront as the strike began. "From Portland, Maine, to Hampton Roads, Virginia, and all the Gulf ports," Corridan wrote, "the fate of 60,000 men hangs in the balance these days. The men who break out or stow away the cargoes of foreign trade in the iron bellies of ships are in trouble, and it's serious."

CHAPTER 12

ABOVE THE FOLD

The newspaper Joe Ryan held in his hands had raised quite a bit of noise on its way around his union offices. Normally Ryan considered the Republican *Sun* an old-guard anti-labor sheet beneath his contempt, but he could not easily dismiss the offensive phrase smearing today's front page: CRIME ON THE WATERFRONT. The thick black letters announced that an exposé series would show how "Mobsters, Linked to Vast International Crime Syndicate, Rule New York Piers by Terror and Harvest Millions." The writer was in fact the same fellow who'd visited Ryan's office with a notebook full of accusations. From the look of today's paper, Johnson had emerged from their encounter undissuaded: The waterfront, he claimed, had "become a veritable haven for ex-convicts" who found and held control "through the unions, particularly the powerful International Longshoremen's Association." Ryan read with disgust that his proud docks were no better than an "outlaw frontier" where "criminal gangs operate with apparent immunity from the law. These gangs are well organized and their control of the piers absolute. Their greatest weapon is terror, invoked by their strong-arm squads and their gunmen. Their power is such that they are able to levy tribute on every pound of cargo arriving at this port." The paper somehow estimated that $50 million a year was lost in "systematic thievery" and promised future articles would show that the dock racketeers were linked to a national crime "syndicate" that stitched together criminal outfits in "every major city of this country."

That Monday's *Sun* also made a heavy landing at the offices of the Manhattan district attorney, Frank Hogan, in the Criminal Courts building attached to the Tombs. The amount of information lifted from his own staff files—reports from his Rackets Bureau on gangsters in the longshore union, background on old murder cases from his Homicide Bureau—angered the normally even-tempered prosecutor, who was all too accustomed to seeing his office's work exploited without attribution by politicians. Johnson seemed extremely well informed, and yet the ungrateful drift of his investigation appeared to be that nothing effective was being done against waterfront crime by Hogan's office or by local police. This was close to the opinion of his source in the office, Assistant DA Bill Keating, who had introduced Johnson to a few cooperative dockers met through his own investigations and allowed him access to crucial files. "Murder on the waterfront is commonplace, a logical product of widespread gangsterism," Johnson wrote, while pilferage was so rampant it amounted to an unofficial national tax. "Losses from theft . . . are easily three times greater than in all other American ports combined." In 1948, one steamship company, the Grace Line, had "suffered losses of about $3,000,000, 80 percent of which disappeared from its New York piers."

Johnson had drawn a disturbing new portrait of the port, charting the many mobster holdings along the docks and linking them directly to the large-scale political corruption that made it all possible. Hogan, while sharing many of the same suspicions, demanded to know how Johnson had learned so much. When it reached Bill Keating that his boss was "fit to be tied" over the sensational articles and wanted to know "Is Johnson getting information from our files?" Keating tried to smooth things over by brokering a belated interview in the *Sun* between Hogan and Johnson.

Word of the crime series brought disgust to McGrath men eating chops in the West Shore Bar and Grill and to the Bowers men shaking down truckers at North River Pier 88. In Brooklyn, Johnson's charges angered Camarda bosses picking their crews along Columbia Street. The crime stories even made their way up the Hudson to the death house at Sing Sing, where Cockeye Dunn had just gained another stay of execution from Governor Dewey. What the *Sun* staff called "Mike's Soup" had come to a high boil, and his investigation had finally reached what he called "the rank-and-file mobsters." There were more menacing voices now calling Johnson's house, growling threats on his life or his family into the phone, but they came too late.

The fresh round of thuggish calls was soon balanced out by grateful messages and crime tips from ordinary pier workers, for whom the stories brought a shock of recognition. "You're getting near the stuff," a half-century veteran of the Hoboken docks told Johnson by phone after the first articles appeared. "Look out for two fellows named William (Bill) Corbett . . . and Charlie Anderson. They're a couple of rats. They play both ends, like a rubber band." The responses came from dockers who'd taken loans from waterfront sharks to get hired, or who'd lost out in the shape to men dressed in code—a red shirt, a toothpick behind the ear— advertising their willingness to kick back; from checkers who had watched cargo routinely diverted; or from haulers sick of the threats and payoffs that went with delivering their load. In West Side places such as Pop's Pier Tavern, they were quietly cheering on this attack on "Dime Joe" and his band. A checker called to tell Johnson about a particularly "hot" West Side pier run by the Dunn gang. "The gangsters wouldn't let me stay there because I was honest . . . Look into the thievery there. I know for a fact that 15,000 cases of spaghetti were stolen there only recently."

The extra calls about the series bounced waterfront stories all around the city room. "I'm a trucker, see, running up and down between New York and the South," a caller told the city desk's Dave Snell. "I just hit town two days ago and I seen the stories you've been carrying. I'm a Southerner and I don't like to be cheated on my load by these New York rackets. . . . My name? It wouldn't be safe for me to tell it to you." The *Sun*'s Dan Anderson, whose normal fare as a television columnist ran to reviews of *Break the Bank* and *School of Tomorrow*, took a message for Johnson from "One of your friends, distinguished by his anonymity and gravelly voice[, who] today had this to grate":

> I see where Mr. Johnson said a private detective called up and said he was right about the loading racket. If that was the McRoberts Agency, they're the worst thieves on the waterfront, and that includes Mr. McRoberts himself . . . I used to work for them, and I know. I'm a checker now. McRoberts is in with all the thieves.

The copyboy Les Woodcock barely knew Mike Johnson to say hello to when an "unidentified source" called from some-where on the waterfront offering him "two men you might be able to get something on." The first was Teddy Gleason, "official for a checkers union . . . collector for all loading rackets in N.Y.C. and

Jersey. . . . comes to N.Y. about once a month . . . starts at Pier 91 and when finished in N.Y.C. goes over to Hoboken and Jersey City." The other candidate, claimed the source, was the Tammany pol Frank Sampson, brother of the Chelsea ILA leader Gene Sampson. "You can get to him and he can be pushed."

CHAPTER 13

JUST STRANGERS

The morning gathered slowly in a drizzle around the harbor to the sounds of buoy whistles and foghorns. Despite the murk that sat over the West Side docks, John Corridan was in a state of rising exuberance as the morning shape-up whistles drilled. The first of Mike Johnson's stories had appeared like a bolt on November 8; now Corridan was finishing his own article endorsing the wildcat strike he remained sure was coming despite assurances in the papers of a last-minute deal. Today's *Times* story drew a call from Father Corridan's editor at *America*, Benjamin Masse, S.J., who regretted that the magazine could no longer use his article, given that the strike had been averted. "Ben," Corridan insisted, "that's what the *Times* thinks but it's not what the men think; they are already slipping off the piers."

The two priests returned to their original plan of running Corridan's story with a "pre-note" about the impending showdown. On Wednesday morning the steady rain kept many cargo hatches shut, adding to the look of growing abandonment along the Chelsea waterfront as locals considered whether to walk or obey the whistle. Corridan and his docker friends rushed from the printer's to begin leafletting the West Side, spreading thousands of runoffs of his appeal, "Longshoremen's Case," along the pierheads and in maritime diners and saloons both pro- and anti-Ryan: "If ratification should fail, the entire Atlantic coast may be in for one of the costliest periods of industrial strife in its history," he warned, echoing what he'd told Cyrus Ching in Washington. "The heart of the matter is the system of hiring along the waterfront. Men are hired as if they were beasts of burden, part of the slave market of a pagan era." In this world of the docks with its fearful code,

> A man does not complain against the impositions and levies that people two blocks inland would find an intolerable racket.
>
> Men have to work. The game has been played that way since the piers jutted out into the River.
>
> If a longshoreman can't keep straight, and yet can't make good at a "racket," drink comes easy. He succumbs to the loan sharks and the installment hawks. To get himself out of their clutches he needs to make a "killing."

As the revolt he'd predicted grew throughout the long, wet day, Corridan's rebel friends littered the waterfront with his remarks, which ended: "The cause of the men of the docks, the hard-muscled, honorable men whose work means so much to our daily living, is a challenging call to all Christians. For these men are our brothers, redeemed in the precious blood of Christ, and one cannot rest secure if His dignity in them continues to be violated and outraged."

In Brooklyn, many dockers laughed at the eight o'clock shape-up whistle that morning, and six thousand of them walked off the piers and into nearby diners and bars. But the center of the emerging strike was, appropriately enough, Joe Ryan's old Chelsea Local 791, which was now run, as many felt the larger union would one day be, by John J. "Gene" Sampson. Sampson had led out his men in the 1945 challenge to Ryan, whose job he coveted, and when later asked to describe their fractious relationship, he smiled: "Just strangers, let's say." Of this latest strike, Gene explained, "Our fellows' demands are simple. They want eight hours work, eight hours play, and eight hours sleep, and they want at least $16 a day to do it with." Unlike other would-be contenders for the ILA's presidency, Sampson could compete with Ryan in powerful circles beyond the waterfront—his own political friendships in Tammany and City Hall gave him nerve. As Ryan well knew, Sampson's brother, Frank, had recently served as Tammany leader with the political help of Mayor O'Dwyer. But while Gene Sampson aspired to run the union, he didn't mean to reform it so much as make himself boss. Sampson carried his local's membership information, he said, Ryan-like, "under my hat."

Between Johnson's siege in the paper and the growing defections of his men, Ryan was defending attacks on two fronts, fumbling for a way to hit back, when the second *Sun* article delivered on the paper's promise that readers would "Meet the Boys" from the rackets. A brooding group of them were posed in dark right profile across the front page—Mickey Bowers, Tim O'Mara, John "Keefie" Keefe, Johnny Applegate, and John Ward. "Each gang rules a territory and rules it with an iron hand, its power enforced by killers and strong-arm squads," Johnson wrote. Then, starting with the late Thomas Collentine's North River Pier 92, he took readers on a grim tour of the crime territories that shaded the shoreline of Manhattan and Brooklyn.

The Bowers Gang had the run of the piers above 42nd Street, including the ILA's "Pistol Local" 824; lower down the island, Tim

O'Mara's gang presided over the Chelsea District between Forty-second and Fourteenth; the Dunn-McGrath territory picked up at Anthony Hintz's former Pier 51 and extended down to Cedar Street; making the Battery Park turn at the bottom of the island, the lower Manhattan piers appeared, still commanded (from prison) by "Socks" Lanza and his "representatives," Johnson's sources claimed, along with the Fulton Fish Market, whose protection rackets had been the center of his power. Swinging up the East River toward the bridges, the tour ended with the South Brooklyn docks run by Albert Anastasia and his brother in the ILA, "Tough Tony" Anastasio. The next time readers boarded a West Side steamship or bought fruit that had come through the Chelsea docks or fish from the Fulton Market, they would think about the grafty, violent network of gangs and rackets they'd paid extra to support.

In that same edition, Johnson's informant "Joe," who now feared for his life after refusing to commit murder for one of his bosses, described the violent ascendance of the Bowers gang on the West Side following the death of the union delegate Richard Gregory: "There was a fight for power on the upper West Side. Suddenly a new mob walked in and took over. That was the Bowers mob, and I started paying dues to these boys." Among other things, the Bowers group now ran its Allied Stevedoring Corporation, which Bill Keating had recently characterized in court as "a front for the loading rackets" and whose husky, overconfident president, John Ward, Johnson had met outside a Manhattan courthouse the previous spring when the 245-pound Ward offered him a bribe to keep his name out of print: "'Go buy yourself a smoke,' Ward said, handing the reporter a ten-dollar bill. The reporter returned the money. Ward then tried to stuff the bill in the reporter's coat. The reporter again returned it and Ward shrugged and walked away with his attorney."

On the afternoon of November 9, one of Johnson's contacts in the Bowerses' territory, Johnny Clinton, an assistant hiring boss and loan shark on Pier 90, was sufficiently impressed by the crime series' debut to call and warn Johnson to keep his name "out of them pieces." Clinton had nevertheless given up the name of his boss on the pier, an ex-convict whose many arrests included grand larceny, robbery, and homicide. In two days of his waterfront series, Johnson had roughly laid out the port's criminal hunting grounds and brought annoying publicity to one of its controlling mobs. He wasn't nearly done.

CHAPTER 14

COMMUNISTS AND NEWSMEN

Ryan was still furious and off-balance when he finally struck back, trying to stitch all his bad news together and build a coalition of the insulted. Having backed the unpopular contract and darkly hinted that only Communists in his union favored a strike, he now blamed the entire walkout on the ambitions of a scandal-mongering newsman:

> This sudden strike was caused by the articles of Malcolm Johnson, which began in The Sun on Monday, while we were negotiating. It was a written insult to our members. It is a serious factor in this strike. The articles tend to show our union is a front for these rackets. It is a direct insult to the Police Commissioner and the FBI. We are ready to be investigated at any time.

By the time the longshoremen began to walk out, local by local, without their "lifetime" president, the shipping news editor George

Horne had been a Ryan watcher for more than twenty years. Horne had come to New York from Oklahoma in the twenties and joined the *Times* the same year Ryan took control of the union, 1927. On the afternoon of the walkout's first day, he was one of a group of reporters and television cameramen waiting for Ryan to speak at an Atlantic Council meeting on the West Side. Over a period of hours, Ryan's pose was fast evolving from calling the shippers' offer a "fine deal" to standing beside his challenger, Gene Sampson, in a clumsy show of unity.

Horne watched Ryan "comb his thinning hair as he mounted the platform before which the cameras were being set up"; then Ryan warmed his audience with an attack on the Fair Labor Standards Act and the union's botched press coverage, especially those lurid stories everyone had read in the *Sun*. "We have been investigated from away back before many of you guys were born," he bragged, "and they had nothing on us." Then, Horne observed, Ryan broke with unity altogether and testily remarked that "investigators ought to turn to 'the insurance partnership of Frank Sampson,' " the Tammany politician and brother of the ILA man sharing the stage with him, Gene Sampson. "Mr. Sampson, white-faced, shouted at his president to 'retract everything you said about my brother!' " noted George Horne. " 'You retract it or we'll make you retract it!' " As voices rose and reporters took excited notes, Sampson showed his own debating skills by accusing Ryan of being unseemly "partners" with the Manhattan borough president, Hugo Rogers, and the radical East Harlem congressman Vito Marcantonio. The "bitter and inelegant words" continued to fly until Ryan recovered enough to try to ring down the curtain and move the family argument out of earshot. "Get out," he commanded the stageful of baffled press. "We are going into executive session."

The next day, as grounded cargo began to mount and passenger ships were stranded around the harbor, Ryan and Sampson were no closer to reading from the same script. Hours after Sampson darkly predicted to reporters that union tug men would join their strike, crippling deliveries of the city's fuel oil, Ryan shot back, "Whoever made that statement is belittling our organization. We will not need to hurt citizens of New York to carry on this strike and there is no need to alarm them at this time." The strike had so far caused mail and rail shipments to pile up, and hundreds of steamship passengers had lugged or wheeled what they could of their baggage while liners such as the *Britannic* and the *Veendam* and a ship carrying the Wright Brothers' Kitty Hawk to the Smithsonian were diverted to Nova Scotia. When the big red, white, and blue stacks of the *America* sailed into view, reporters gathered to watch the actress Helen Hayes make her homecoming without longshoremen. She struggled down the gangway with her load, noted George Horne, then sent her husband, the writer Charles MacArthur, on board to retrieve the rest, while the circus executive John Ringling North was forced to leave his car in the ship's hold.

Three days in, Joe Ryan formally joined the strike that Gene Sampson seemed to be leading. Although the movement had already spread to Philadelphia and Baltimore, Ryan called out forty-five thousand East Coast members from Maine to Virginia, regardless of how their locals had voted on the contract. But declaring his union's first official strike had not gained Ryan control.

Each day's Johnson article raised a fresh scandal from the waterfront. He'd made a stab at the Bowers gang; next he described the brutal loading rackets through the story of the rise of Varick Enterprises, organized during Prohibition by Cockeye Dunn and others. It had served as a front for dock rackets on a "pretentious scale," Johnson disclosed, its fees "collected by squads of goons" and its innovations including sophisticated blackmail schemes, according to a Mob accountant named "Charlie M":

> While doing this work, Charlie learned that some of the truckmen were keeping two sets of books, one set showing the actual condition of their companies, the other falsified for tax purposes. . . . Varick evolved as a medium by which the truckmen could be blackmailed as the price for silence on their income tax evasion.

One of Varick's union offices had been in the same Eighth Avenue building with Joe Ryan's ILA.

Just after dawn on the morning of November 15, Mayor William O'Dwyer's plane approached New York after flying through the night from California. The longshoremen's walkout, although legalized by O'Dwyer's friend Joe Ryan, had called him home a week into his vacation, the fourth of his term scuttled by strike since O'Dwyer emerged from the army a brigadier general and became mayor in the fall of 1945.

His own history with the waterfront had disturbed his first days as mayor-elect when he was brought back to Brooklyn Central Courthouse to face a grand jury called by his Republican replacement, who among other things charged "gross laxity" in office for O'Dwyer's failure to prosecute the man he had once bragged he had a "perfect" murder case against, Albert Anastasia. O'Dwyer spent more than eleven hours on the stand over three days, explaining that whatever case once existed against Anastasia had gone "out the window" when his star witness in the Murder Inc. trials, Abe "Kid Twist" Reles, fell from a Coney Island hotel window. Nevertheless, the grand jury returned with a tough presentment that December of 1945: "We find that the proof against Anastasia was neglected, disregarded, and deposited in the office files and vaults until prosecution was barred by the Statute of Limitations."

The grand jury's words were quickly forgotten by the public as more current events claimed the new mayor's attention. When the Port of New York was closed by striking tugboat operators in 1946, O'Dwyer had declared a state of emergency that closed the city from stem to stern—emptying all bars, museums, theaters, and libraries while cops posted at subway stations turned away all but emergency riders. After eighteen hours of citywide panic, though, he lifted the drastic order. "I just didn't know anything about city government," he later confessed. "Everybody thinks he could be mayor, and I thought so too. But it's a job that takes a lot of learning. . . . Any fool learns something in time."

By November 1948, the mayor's job had forced an impressive amount of learning on him. Now, as the sun rose, he assembled his options flying above the quieted Hudson riverfront where he'd once worked as a brawny young immigrant. The harbor was set with lines of dock-bound ships, its piers piled untidily here and there with abandoned loads—crates, oil drums, steel—the water open except where a car float or ferry cut it. When he landed at LaGuardia Field and made his way to City Hall, O'Dwyer returned to a city that had been outraged since his departure by the revelations in a newspaper crime series—today's installment featured the wiretapped banter of a New York "loading racket gang." As he would throughout the weeks of the series' run, O'Dwyer had the *Sun* articles clipped and sent on to his deeply annoyed police commissioner. But the Johnson stories were already kicking around dozens of offices, spreading shock and recrimination, panic and relief, through corridors from New York's criminal courts to City Hall to Albany and Washington.

CHAPTER 15

THE PEACEMAKER

With his three-piece British suits and dark wispy mustache, Bill Margolis reminded strangers more of the English movie star Ronald Colman than of what reporters called an "ace labor peacemaker." Wherever he went for the Federal Mediation and Conciliation Service, dispatched to a crisis of angry machinists, telegraph operators, or Merchant Seamen, his arrival meant the talks' outcome had some national import—enough to call in help from the Washington big leagues.

Margolis spent a busy part of the fall of 1948 in San Francisco, in the thick of the poisonous standoff between Harry Bridges's dock militants and West Coast shippers. He arrived there with some unusual private instructions from Ohio's Republican senator Robert Taft, the stolid, bespectacled power broker who had just lost his party's nomination to the dynamic former crime fighter Thomas Dewey. The Taft-Hartley labor act was central to the current dispute on the West Coast, and like Joe Ryan, Taft took an almost obsessive interest in the uncontrollable man Margolis was on his way to meet.

The Aussie Harry Bridges claimed that his boyhood fondness for the scratch-and-claw world of Jack London had drawn him to the maritime life and eventually to America, where he would found his International Longshore and Warehouse Union; by the time Bill Margolis met with him, he had already survived two federal deportation trials as an accused Communist and further antagonized shipowners by refusing to sign Taft-Hartley's non-Communist oath. At the same time, Bridges was infuriated by the act's prohibition against the closed-shop hiring halls his union had used to replace the shape-up. He laid in for a long strike in early September, swearing his workers would unload no cargoes except the bodies of returning servicemen: "Only the dead will be worked."

As Margolis later told it, Senator Taft instructed him to stick with Bridges and observe him carefully for subversive signs. Luckily, "The Nose" had a fun side when out of sight of steamship executives, which Margolis learned while keeping up with him after hours around San Francisco while negotiations were otherwise stalled. In a bar, with a cigarette flopping in the corner of his mouth and completing his sharp, bony profile, Bridges skewered his many well-deserved enemies into the night. He prided himself on his dangerous reputation as a lefty belligerent, and finally asked, according to Bill's son, the political reporter Jon Margolis, "Aren't you taking a chance spending so much time with me? I'm kind of an unsavory character."

Margolis answered confidently, "Senator Taft wants me to keep an eye on you. If anybody asks me, I'll just tell them I'm cooperating with Bob Taft. What's more anti-Communist than that?" Anyone who could deal professionally with both the conservative Taft and the fiery Bridges surely had a bombproof kind of personality and considerable mediating skills. But things remained so bad in the strike, positions dug in so deep, that representatives could not be coaxed into the same room over its first ten weeks.

Margolis made a return visit to San Francisco in early November and found that attitudes had softened enough for both sides to accept his offer of a "peace meeting." Then, having finally primed the pump for discussions out west, he went home to Washington and, on the night of November 16, received a call from the service's regional director in New York, warning that the East Coast strike had reached its own crisis. Joe Ryan had attempted to block hundreds of rank-and-file longshoremen from gathering at the Manhattan Center and rallying to seek payment under the Supreme Court's recent ruling on their back pay claims. Ryan's group greeted them with flyers charging that the meeting had been convened by the Communist Party to attack his union and disrupt Marshall Plan shipments to Europe. "If the Communists interfere," Ryan pledged, "our men will throw them in the river." According to the *Times*'s George Horne, Ryan's name was "booed lustily" by the eight hundred dockers inside the hall; then the raucous night closed reverently with a bowing of heads for Peter Panto, who was almost ten years gone.

The day after receiving his call, Bill Margolis flew to New York, where he'd last been sent to defuse a near strike by telegraph workers. The entry into the mix of this "crack labor peacemaker" from Washington made a hopeful counterpoint on the *Sun*'s front page to Mike Johnson's darkly expert discussion of how "Pay-roll Padding, Kickbacks, Usury, Payoffs and Contributions Yield Harvest for Dock Mobs." Whether or not Johnson was responsible for Joe Ryan's recent troubles, he might as well have been, as the *Sun* articles continued to stir anarchic feelings roiling around the harbor. "The longshoreman in New York has no security," Johnson wrote. "In his eagerness for work he is easy prey for the racketeers and grafting union officials." As Margolis got his bearings, *Sun* readers learned how Social Security numbers were filed under fictitious names to create ghost workers whose pay went back to New York mobsters; and about loan sharks such as Frank Savio, a boss checker in the ILA convicted of running a ring that made $200,000 per year:

> He was lending money to the longshoremen and charging them 10 cents a week on the dollar. It was shown that Savio was able to have the interest due him deducted from the longshoremen's pay before they received it thanks to the co-operation of pay clerks. On the occasion of a previous arrest, when Savio was charged with assault, Joseph P. Ryan . . . appeared as a character witness in his behalf.

Johnson quoted an informant from the Bowerses' West Side piers describing the tradition of "voluntary" contributions demanded every payday, and what happened to dockers who neglected to drop a dollar into the cigar box: "He might refuse once, and maybe nothing would happen to him. But then again something might. He might find he couldn't get work, or he might get kicked around. A man soon got the idea: he didn't refuse more than once."

These portraits of widely tolerated corruption can't have improved the cooperative mood in the rooms where Bill Margolis spent his crowded first days as mediator, sizing up the personalities on all sides of the strike even as Mike Johnson laid out a darker landscape: Margolis met separately with the heads of the Mediation Service's New York office, with the chairman of the New York Shipping Association, John V. Lyon, then with Joe Ryan and the ILA's strike committee. He found a president who was battling in several directions at once.

By Thursday, when Margolis saw the mayors of Jersey City and New York at City Hall, the growing strike had stranded ships in

Boston, Philadelphia, Baltimore, Portland (Maine), and Norfolk, Virginia; traveled the Hudson to tie up grain ships in the state capital at Albany; diverted many big liners to Canada; and laid off scores of city truckers and hundreds of rail freight handlers in New Jersey and New Haven. The Midtown hotels were crammed with ocean-bound tourists waiting to sail, while large cargoes of bananas and chestnuts ripened uselessly at dockside. Tens of thousands of mail bags had already piled up, and another twenty thousand tons of Marshall Plan goods went undelivered each day. "The service is neither optimistic nor pessimistic," Margolis cautioned reporters. "Remember, we settled this once . . . and it blew up. Now we've got to go out and settle it again." After a long day mediating at the Hotel Edison near Times Square, Margolis served weary notice on all parties: "We're prepared to get into this session and stay in this session until we drop dead." Over the weekend, the strike crossed the Atlantic to Southampton, England, where the crew of the *Queen Elizabeth*—citing solidarity as well as fear of reprisal from their brothers if they landed at New York—walked off with two thousand guests waiting to sail.

CHAPTER 16

OUR WIT'S END

For Governor Thomas Dewey, reading about the scandals of the waterfront recalled one area that—except for the Savio loan-sharking conviction Johnson cited—had largely escaped his gang-busting during his dashing career as Manhattan district attorney. Even as he read Johnson's continued assault on Johnny Dunn, Tom Dewey knew a good deal about the stray-eyed, bantamweight crime leader, having so far granted him five stays of execution. Dunn remained in Sing Sing, following the progress of his newest appeal, while Johnson described the stubborn rise and ten-year reign that helped put him there—an unromantic climb built on small, ruthless steps (such as his elimination of a Seventeenth Street pier boss named Johnny Costello as he pushed a baby carriage). One waterfront investigator explained Dunn's "technique" for Johnson:

> The modern gangster and labor racketeer doesn't bother to organize the men into a union. He first gets a union charter. Anybody

can get one. Then, if his organization is powerful enough, he goes directly to the employers and demands a "contract." When he gets the contract, he informs the workmen they are now in his union— or else.

Aspiring to control from the piers inland to the freight terminals, Dunn created the Motor and Bus Terminal Checkers, Platform and Office Workers and got charters for three locals from the AFL. With himself as union president, and his gunman Andy Sheridan an organizer in his Jersey local, Dunn hoped to poach on the rackets territory held by the pier boss Charlie "the Jew" Yanowsky. "In time," wrote Johnson, "Dunn's union controlled the checkers and platform workers at some 168 inland freight terminals where his union had contracts."

Governor Dewey knew more than Johnson did about Dunn's wartime career and perplexing influence in Washington, but was sworn to secrecy, as a later government report would show. In 1943, Dunn was prosecuted for coercion for blocking two British convoys while attempting to take a West Village pier. A political campaign began almost immediately following his arrest, led by officials in the War Department and the Transportation Corps's Colonel Frederick C. Horner, who wrote to the parole board of Dunn's vital role in "preventing the spread of what might very well be serious labor disturbances, and also in the adjustment of these disturbances." Horner added, "consideration of the factors mentioned above and many others which I am not at liberty to divulge compel the decision to ask for his immediate release from your care and custody." The Parole Commission was unanimously convinced and voted to free Dunn the next day, February 4, 1943, infuriating Mayor La Guardia, for whom a thug remained a thug in peace or war, and who successfully fought to have Dunn's release reversed.

In citing this evidence, Johnson ascribed Dunn's Washington

influence to his membership in a possible "super crime syndicate." "The full results of the high-pressure intervention in Dunn's case by the Army brass," he wrote, "probably will never be known to the public." It wasn't for almost thirty years that documents declassified by Thomas Dewey's estate revealed the strange chapter of governmental enlistment of waterfront gangsters in the war effort.

With the popular fear that followed Pearl Harbor and the spectacular burning of the converted liner *Normandie* at its midtown pier, Johnny Dunn, Lucky Luciano, Meyer Lansky, and Socks Lanza were secretly approached by the Office of Naval Intelligence to help secure New York Harbor against port sabotage and submarine attack. For two years, navy investigators relied on the persuasion and intelligence gathering of the harbor's leading mobsters; Lanza found himself in charge of recruiting area fishermen to join his submarine watch and collect tips about possible sabotage.

As for Cockeye Dunn's security role, Meyer Lansky told a government interviewer:

> Dunn's job was to be a watchdog on the piers, to have trusted employees amongst the loaders, to make friends with the crews, and to stay with them to get reports if there was any bad men around the crowd. . . . He also got friends along the waterfront in the bar rooms. If any of the crews got drunk, and they would talk something that you would feel is subversive, to report to him.

When Dunn later flirted with exposing New York politicians to save himself from the electric chair, his strange wartime service was the least of the secrets at his disposal.

After four grinding days of talks, Bill Margolis returned briefly to Washington on Sunday, November 21, 1948, to strategize with his lanky patrician boss, Cyrus Ching. "Mediators," Ching believed, "have learned long ago that . . . there is no substitute for the seemingly endless drudgery of prolonged discussion, persistent persuasion, and reasonable argument." But if these tools failed, Ching was not above using a little trickery to give the talks a "nudge." Neither man wanted this strike to become as drawn out and heated as the West Coast standoff. "We were all at our wit's end as to what to do," Ching recalled.

The Washington labor men worked up a new approach to the impasse: Ching sent a pair of telegrams to prepare the way for his own arrival in New York. The first cable went to Ryan, a "very likeable sort of chap," Ching said years later. "He would always talk very freely and frankly about 'legitimate graft.' He really could see nothing wrong with taking a bribe." (Ching had heard often from Ryan earlier in the contract talks, and when a strike was first threatened by Ryan's men, Joe made an urgent call to Ching's Washington office to plead, "Hurry up with that injunction, because I can't hold these fellows any longer.") Ching's second telegram went to the New York Shipping Association's chairman, John V. Lyon. Ching instructed both men to meet him at the Hotel Edison at 9:00 a.m. that coming Wednesday.

Surrounded by the Deco touches of the Edison, the two sides were still stymied over a pay raise and welfare fund, unaware they'd been invited to a kind of poker round, when Ching arrived that morning to play the government's sneaky hand: "Gentlemen, I just want to deliver a very short message to you. If you do not assure me by four o'clock this afternoon that you have made substantial progress in the way of a settlement of this difficulty, the federal government is going to take action." When both men asked what exactly the government might do, Ching's answer was clipped: "I will tell you at four o'clock." Ching's title and formal manners perhaps disguised the hollowness of his threat, since one federal injunction had already failed to spur a solution. At eleven that morning, Ryan phoned to ask for an extension, and Ching moved the deadline to 6:00 p.m., then repeated the offer when Lyon called at noon, panicked that he couldn't round up all his voting members in time. Then Ching smoked his pipe and waited.

Under pressure of Ching's murky threat, the two men reported back with "substantial" progress late that afternoon. Ching urged them to "keep it up," and a long, complex night emerged, with mediators shuttling among three conference rooms at the Edison— one holding the 125 members of the wage scale committee, another for a mixed group of union and shipping men, and a louder room full of dozens of longshoremen who rotated in and out of the nearby bar. Proposals and counterproposals moved from one room to another until, according to Bill Margolis's official report, an offer was finally accepted at 3:35 on Thanksgiving morning. Gene Sampson, whose men of Local 791 had been among the first to walk off the piers more than two weeks earlier, offered a resolution that the union committee give the mediators "a rising vote of thanks."

When Harry Truman met with his head mediator days later at the White House, he congratulated Ching on the negotiation's dramatic end. Ching credited the government's use of an unspecified threat to both parties, leading Truman to ask, "What did you have in mind?"

"Well, you're a better poker player than I am, Mr. President," Ching said, gracefully downplaying his and Margolis's accomplishment at the Edison. "I tried a good bluff and it worked."

CHAPTER 17

TO SPEAK WITHOUT FEAR

As Joe Ryan's union again prepared to vote, Mike Johnson's target shifted to "a tall, well-dressed man with light gray eyes and brown hair, who lives at a midtown hotel and directs his operations with quiet efficiency." Ed McGrath, forty-two, had survived the prosecution of his criminal business partner and brother-in-law Cockeye Dunn by tending more toward the executive style than toward "open violence." Dunn and McGrath had each come to the waterfront in the middle 1930s through the social network of Sing Sing prison, but McGrath did not have a childhood typical of his fellow gangsters, Johnson observed, and "made the grade from choirboy to big-time mobster by diligently applying himself to the business of crime." His reward was control of the busy piers from Fourteenth Street down to Cedar. Cockeye Dunn, who had recently complained to a prison snitch that he was only in the death house because Andy Sheridan's gun had jammed, now had to read how his cleverer brother-in-law had "taken over" the gang's operations "in name as well as in fact."

With strikes in the process of being settled on both coasts, several hundred Brooklyn holdouts rallied over the weekend of the union vote to stoke the last coals of the revolt against Ryan. Jim Longhi, whose Brooklyn law office served as headquarters for the largest of the back pay committees, had lately felt an increased level of menace from gangsters he saw around Red Hook. "They knew who we were, we knew them," he said years later. By inviting the mayor's brother, Paul O'Dwyer, to chair a meeting of the Brooklyn strikers, Longhi hoped to gain a skilled and sympathetic labor lawyer who might also draw the group better police protection. He got both when, after some hesitation, O'Dwyer joined the dying rebellion.

Paul O'Dwyer was the last in a line of eleven children in which Bill O'Dwyer had been the first. Growing up in Ireland, he had never seen his much older brother until he made landfall in America in 1925 and savored his first strawberry soda. Paul was twenty-eight when he entered the gauntlet of immigrant jobs that Bill, now a Brooklyn attorney, had passed through years earlier. As a checker on the docks, Paul faithfully followed the code book and reported the first pilferage he witnessed: he was quickly fired. He soon came to the law himself, and got another view of the waterfront's criminal coloration while serving as a lawyer for some Camarda locals in 1940, when his brother was the Brooklyn DA. Bill had come to America to leave Ireland; his younger brothers left Ireland to join him. While Bill refused to send money home, his brothers loyally did so in his name. "Paul was a progressive," remembered Jim Longhi, whose dock experiences allowed him to distinguish between the brothers O'Dwyer. "He could do selfless things to help the underdog. I can't say the same for Bill."

For his first meeting with the rebel docker group in Red Hook in 1948, Paul O'Dwyer prepared a short, earnest talk in tourist Italian. It was a speech he had rehearsed with Longhi as a way to introduce himself and announce that a "new day" had come to the waterfront:

> I'd learned the lesson well and was able to say in Italian as well as in English, "This is a new day. The day of the gangster telling you you can't speak is finished. This is emancipation day for the Italian longshoremen in Brooklyn, and you are not to be bound by these thugs any longer. . . . Freedom of speech has come to the waterfront, where a man may speak without fear."

When he had finished, he looked hopefully across his broad-shouldered audience. A rough, commanding voice soon rose from the back: " 'Mister, why, you mean anybody can go up there and speak?' And I said, 'That's what I said.' He said, 'You mean I can go up there and speak?' And I said, 'That's what I mean. Come on up.' "

There was a hush—out of respect or fear—as a stocky, big-chested man with graying close-cropped hair stalked through the crowd to grip the microphone like a baton. "My name is Anthony Anastasio," "Tough Tony" himself barked into the mike, and a chilly kind of order clamped over the gathering. Emancipation Day was over.

Paul O'Dwyer was back in Brooklyn leading rallies by the hold-outs against ratification, as ILA men voted all along the Atlantic seaboard finally to approve their contract. "The men don't have a fair chance to express themselves in this union," O'Dwyer said to six hundred gathered in Brooklyn's St. Stephen's Hall as the last votes were tallied. After some loud arguments, he prevailed upon the men to respect the election results and return to work. At the request of the mayor, work resumed on the docks the next morning, a Sunday, to rescue whatever could be saved from rotting. Joe Ryan toured the North River piers as his men again entered the morning shape-up and noise returned to the waterfront.

Despite the national relief that followed news of the settlement, Mike Johnson kept the waterfront's criminal side stubbornly in the news. The mayor had all along been forwarding the *Sun* stories to his police commissioner, Arthur Wallander, who refused to speak to the reporter. O'Dwyer showed smarter political skills by answering Johnson's questions at the end of November. Then, four days later, in City Hall, he announced the consequences of his uneasy weeks of newspaper reading.

With his commissioner of investigation, John Murtagh, beside him, the mayor declared he was ordering a full inquiry into the dock rackets. "I just got the feeling that there was something wrong there and we should look into it," O'Dwyer told the assembled reporters. However, the scope of the mayor's investigation would start out smaller than the *Sun*'s. In particular, O'Dwyer was frustrated by the city's inability to lease out several of its Greenwich Village piers—an area Johnson had identified as the brutally gained waterfront of the Dunn-McGrath gang—because of local strong-arm tactics and racketeering. The docks investigation would begin there, promised Commissioner Murtagh, and "We will follow it anywhere it leads."

Johnson's crime series was winding down as the city's own investigation lurched into life. After brazenly picturing founders of the Mafia's national commission and charging that the ILA was staffed with scores of ex-convicts, Johnson quoted Joe Ryan's boastful answer to his men: "*The Sun* has been writing about some of the boys from the old ladies' home up the river who came down to the waterfront and made good. I'm proud to have them as members of this union. I'm proud to have my picture taken with them and proud to be in their company."

The editors took Ryan at his word and ran the proudest pictures they could find of Joe smiling at testimonial dinners with his "boys from the old ladies' home," some of whom, such as Johnny Dunn, had since gone back upriver to await their electrocution.

CHAPTER 18

THE MEETING OF MINDS

An angry rumor commanded the West Side riverfront, driven largely by Bowers men, who went from pier to pier like jungle beaters spreading the word before them: the DA had grabbed somebody off the docks and would soon haul in any longshoreman who had an arrest sheet. The messengers visited Midtown docks urging retaliation, and as four hundred workers staged an hour-long walkout, an ILA delegate warned, "We intend to stop every time they take a man away from his work for questioning."

The show of force on December 8 was unknowingly triggered that morning by Mike Johnson's friend in the DA's Homicide Bureau, Bill Keating. Seven months after the hiring boss Thomas Collentine was shot on his way to work, Keating called in a pudgy Bowers functionary named John Potter to discuss the rackets background to the killing. Keating judged Potter to be "an apparently respectable veteran who served as a front in Mickey Bowers' loading activities," and Potter himself was not a suspect. Nevertheless, news immediately leaked about his visit to the Criminal Courts building, Keating remembered, spreading uproar among West Side dockers that "the District Attorney planned to question every long-shoreman who had ever been arrested for anything."

Joe Ryan went into a vintage rage when he heard that Potter had been brought to Keating's office without his permission. He telephoned Keating's surprised boss, Frank Hogan, who at that moment was holding his own press conference about waterfront crime and the charges in the *Sun*. Hogan was understandably annoyed to learn from Ryan about the activities of his staff, but could still crack wise with reporters: "Why, we're always investigating crime on the waterfront. Just a minute ago I got a call from Joe Ryan complaining that one of my assistants is questioning some of his men."

The mayor's dock inquiry, confined at first to three city-owned piers whose dirty reputations left them unrentable, was now actually several investigations, although proceeding with only grudging cooperation from O'Dwyer's police commissioner, Arthur Wallander. When Wallander declined to meet with Mike Johnson or even answer his submitted questions, Johnson published them in an extra story about Wallander's silence. ("What steps are you taking to stamp out crime and racketeering on the water front which, according to our records, has existed for more than thirty years and continues to exist?" "What are your views on the theory . . . that organized crime in New York and elsewhere in the country is directed by a so-called syndicate?") Within weeks, Wallander would leave the Police Department for a quieter job at Con Edison, where no one would ask him about crime syndicates.

On December 10, 1948, Johnson's vivid, scorching, disruptive investigation ended its run, after holding the *Sun*'s front page for more than three dramatic weeks. Ed Bartnett had sent Johnson off into the dock wars months before by handing him the first report of the Collentine shooting. As the long series finally ended, Bart brought over another promising document, a three-page "Open Letter to the New York Sun" signed by two priests at the Xavier labor school, Director Rev. Philip Carey and Associate Director Rev. John Corridan. Johnson had admired Corridan's November article predicting the big ILA strike, "Longshoremen's Case," as had the federal mediators who found copies of it helpfully placed by dockers in their meeting rooms.

"Mike Johnson and the New York Sun are to be congratulated for their real service to the people of New York," the Xavier letter opened, taking to task one of Johnson's interview subjects, a contracting stevedore who had said of the late Jersey docks boss and racketeer Charlie Yanowsky, "Sure, I knew Charlie and I did business with him because he got results. That's what I pay for— results. I am not concerned with how anybody gets them. I'm no reformer. That's the church's business, not mine." The fight against gangsterism was more than church business, Corridan answered, echoing Johnson's conclusion that "the system of hiring and certain other unhealthy practices" made the corruption possible. In Corridan, Johnson found another reformer who lashed into racketeers and Communists with equal zeal. "Every American is opposed to Communism," the priest wrote to the *Sun*, "but it is conditions such as prevail along the docks that promote the cause of Communism, not the American way of life."

Bart handed his reporter the letter with some gentle advice: "You'd better go around and see this man; he seems to know what he's talking about." Having taken on Joe Ryan and the racketeers for weeks in his paper, Johnson headed over to Chelsea to compare notes with the tough character he called the "waterfront priest." Two of Joe Ryan's main irritants would finally share ammunition.

In person, Father Corridan could speak with authority on almost any aspect of the port, from its larger financial picture to its individual tragedies; his knowledge of gang territories and their cast of characters made him both economist and detective. "A razor-edge mind," Mike Johnson noted, "combined with a quick, warm-hearted sympathy and understanding of human frailty." Corridan was also "as tough as they come" and could recite in easy thuggish steps how to take over a pier, or trace how a decent man could fall into perpetual hock, tripped up by the traps set by racketeers. "When he talks of the corruption and the terror against which he is pitted," Johnson later wrote, "the priestly gentleness vanishes from his eyes, leaving only the icy hardness of an outraged Irish-man. . . . [H]is voice and language become again those of a tough, angry West Side kid. When he begins to analyze the classic pattern of waterfront gangsterism, his chain-smoking becomes more com-pulsive, his lip curls, and a realistic bitterness creeps into his voice."

Johnson professed to "no religious preference" but came to be surprised over time at the effect the priest worked on him: "I fan-cied myself as a reasonably hard-bitten reporter, protected by a reporter's carefully assumed insularity. Then somewhere along the line I suddenly woke up to the fact that I was, in effect, one of the Waterfront Priest's 'recruits.' "

The two set to work on a follow-up series for the *Sun*. Both men shared the view that Joe Ryan was essentially a despotic political figure and not a labor leader, and that even his eventual departure from the scene would bring little permanent change to the port if its ancient, grafty hiring system stayed behind. Johnson had laid out the waterfront's many ills for his readers and assigned the blame as he saw it. Next, as the city's docks investigation spun its wheels, he would present solutions in a second round of stories, "Crime on the Waterfront: The Cause and the Remedy."

Dozens of letters continued to reach the city room seconding his findings ("We particularly concur with the article entitled 'The

Loading Racket,' as we have, unfortunately, been forced to pay these loading fees"); the chief challenger was Joe Ryan himself, who wrote in defense of his maligned union and called the writer both a stooge of the Communists and an anti-labor axe grinder "outdoing even the National Association of Manufacturers." (As Johnson pointed out, "I could hardly be both a commy-minded radical and the fair-haired boy of reactionary industrialists.") After reading the *Sun* stories, a group of women from three Brooklyn longshoring families prompted an investigation of Greenpoint loan sharks who were charging yearly interest of more than 500 percent, confiscating borrowers' pay chits and assaulting late payers. Two detectives went undercover as longies to trap the local head of the Brooklyn loan racket.

Grand juries were much in the news as Johnson and Corridan compared notes. The mayor and DA Hogan had publicly argued over the merits of a grand jury approach to the "dock mess," and in mid-December, reporters were chasing secret witnesses through the halls and stairwells of Manhattan's federal courthouse as the grand jury investigating espionage was reconvened in Foley Square. The fierce secrecy around the proceedings forced reporters to guess which courthouse visitors were ordinary New Yorkers and which were anonymous witnesses coming to testify about spies in the government; teams of spotters combed the floors above and below the grand jury room. Even a witness as familiar as Whittaker Chambers, whose soft, fretful face they knew from last summer's congressional spy show, nevertheless proved scrambly and elusive in the long courthouse corridors, a banker's gray figure slipping into stairwells, hat down; "a rotund little man with amazing agility," gasped one weary newsman after days of the chase.

The federal grand jury had reconvened because of evidence Chambers produced in early December from a hollowed-out pumpkin on his Maryland farm. Chambers had been under pressure to back up his claims made in sensational hearings last August that he remembered Alger Hiss as a fellow Communist in a 1930s Washington espionage cell. Chambers asserted that the five rolls of undeveloped film inside his pumpkin were photographic proof of stolen federal documents that Hiss passed to the Soviets during his State Department career. The "pumpkin papers" evidence was brought on loan to New York, jealously guarded by Congressman Richard Nixon, to be shared with the grand jury and then returned to Washington. On Sunday, December 19, as one of New York's heaviest snowfalls settled over the city, it hardly muffled a bitter fight rising out of that week's indictment of Hiss for perjury.

CHAPTER 19

THEY KILL IN THE DARK

Johnson's second series, "Crime on the Waterfront: The Cause and the Remedy," began at the end of January 1949. Rather than merely propose solutions for the port, like a committee report might, he went right back at Joe Ryan and "mobsters in control of the waterfront" for their opposition to hiring halls, used successfully in Seattle, Los Angeles, and Portland since the 1920s. He also chided the Shipping Association for preferring the shape-up system, for all "its waste and inefficiency and demonstrable evils," simply because it delivered labor on the cheap. Johnson answered Ryan's arguments against the hiring hall and analyzed the ILA constitution, which most longshoremen had never seen, as a "blueprint for dictatorship."

Looking beyond the city's docks inquiry, Johnson blamed the longtime political "paralysis" and public indifference toward the waterfront, ending his second round of articles by calling for legislation and a "vigorous, overall state investigation." While some bills had already been introduced in Albany, Johnson clearly had low hopes for the mayor's approach. He cited the observations of the West Side dock "jungle" by an older priest of the waterfront, Staten Island's Father Monaghan:

> The saloons now are hangouts where the men talk from the side of the mouth about deals, cut-ins and dames. . . . In and out of this jungle slink men, bodily different, face shaped the same. The young wolf-eyed, the old rat-faced. These men don't fight, they hunt in packs and kill in the dark. . . . The Mayor of New York, better than most, knows the story of the Judases who sold out the workers. He is kin to the old-timers who split their bodies on the docks. . . . These docks may well be the stumbling block of his political hopes.

Two weeks after the second series ended, a portly reformer appeared outside City Hall to make the same point about the mayor's vulnerability. Wearing a bulky topcoat and light homburg and carrying a hammer in a bag, Clendenin J. Ryan looked pleased by the clutch of newspeople he'd gathered with his promise of a political scandal. A wealthy, middle-aged grandson of the late financier Thomas Fortune Ryan, the younger Ryan had organized a stockholders' group that challenged for control of the International Telephone and Telegraph Corporation the year before. Having lost that public battle, he'd come to the mayor's doorstep with a new target as coordinator for something called the Clean City Government Committee. While insisting he had no ambitions beyond throwing "the bums out," he'd organized this press stunt. Pulling some old photostats from a bag, he began to read righteously aloud: "We have found an abandonment of the waterfront rackets investigation and a complete failure to prosecute the perpetrators of serious crimes although the evidence was admittedly sufficient to require prosecution." Ryan quoted the damning words of a Kings County grand jury's presentment against Bill O'Dwyer from 1945.

The statement he read went on to excoriate O'Dwyer as Brooklyn DA, particularly for his mishandling of the Peter Panto murder case. Ryan pulled a hammer from his bag and nailed the smudgy pages to the city hall door long enough to strike his Martin Luther pose for the cameras. Then he removed his nail, stashed his hammer, and left reporters with a question: "Why does Dewey refuse to investigate O'Dwyer?"

CHAPTER 20

OUT OF THE WOODS

Arthur Miller was bowled over when he first read the New York *Sun*'s unrelenting series on waterfront crime: Day after day came fresh proof of the pay-for-hire schemes and territorial murders that were a rumored part of dock life down the hill from where Miller lived with his family in Brooklyn Heights, on a street overlooking the harbor and its working boats.

He would remember seeing inscrutable Italian messages chalked on his neighborhood walls, the scribbled words (*Dov'è Panto?*) hinting at a closed society down the cobbled slope toward the water. "It was down near the piers that this mysterious question covered every surface," he wrote, "and it was not hard to guess that it was still more evidence of the other world that existed at the foot of peaceful, old-fashioned Brooklyn Heights, the sinister waterfront world of gangster-ridden unions, assassinations, beatings, bodies thrown into the lovely bay at night."

The strange phrase caused Miller to seek the answer among the area's Italian longshoremen, but while he was a gifted playwright, he was no reporter. "It took only a couple of days on the piers to discover that men were afraid to so much as talk about Panto." After several weeks of shy research along the docks, he was forced to admit, "I could never penetrate the permanent reign of quiet terror on the waterfront hardly three blocks from my peaceful apartment."

His problem was bridged when he eventually met Vincent "Jim" Longhi, the gregarious young Red Hook lawyer who had recently run for Congress. Longhi came to serve as Miller's guide through the unfamiliar clamor of the docks, taking the reticent playwright around to the longshore bars and early shape-ups, a scene little changed from Panto's time. "He being an intellectual, who's gonna tell him about the world down the hill from his apartment?" Longhi laughed sixty years later. "The guys called him 'Slim.' They didn't know who he was." Mike Johnson's waterfront series proved more broadly what Miller had heard from Longhi, whose bloody tales of the docks inspired Miller to try his hand at a dramatic work based on the life of Peter Panto.

On May 2, 1949, Miller learned that his current play, a story of a man's tragic but far less heroic destruction, called *Death of a Salesman*, had won the Pulitzer Prize for Best Drama. As proud as he was to win the award, Miller was heartened to see another name whom the Pulitzer Committee, which met at Columbia University, had honored that day. When asked by the newspapers to comment on his achievement, Miller was the only winner to declare that the most deserving name on the Pulitzer list was actually someone else: the *Sun* reporter Malcolm Johnson, whose "Crime on the Waterfront" series had claimed the prize for "Distinguished Local Reporting."

Mike Johnson got his own call that day from Columbia, from a fellow reporter uptown to cover the Pulitzer announcements. When the news of his prize reached the *Sun*, happy bedlam broke out all around its famously reserved city room—stashed bottles and glasses were quickly produced, and a newsroom cocktail party improvised in Mike's honor. "Mike stood, smiling and blushing, properly proud but with innate modesty making him look almost sheepish, in the center of a ring of pleased co-workers," Dan Anderson wrote of his friend in the *Sun*. "It was several minutes before he could break away to telephone his wife."

With two college tuitions and a new baby son, the Johnson house would put the five-hundred-dollar prize to quick use, but as Millie Branham remembered, Mike had trouble at first even reaching anyone with his news. "It was a really hot story and he couldn't go anywhere with it." When Bill Heinz eventually worked his way through the friendly huddle to congratulate Johnson at his desk, he found him "on the phone trying to reach his daughter saying, 'Please tell her I have won the Pulitzer Prize, that's P as in Peter, U as in union . . .' " Haynes Johnson was a freshman at the University of Missouri when he received an excited telephone call from his mother: "It was great, and I particularly recall the pleasure I got in reading the articles about his winning in the next day's *St. Louis Post-Dispatch* and the *Kansas City Star*."

Johnson had already won the Women's Press Club's Merit Award earlier in the year, declaring, "It is the task of reporters to penetrate iron curtains wherever they may be, even on the New York waterfront." About this latest prize, he was less Olympian: "Look, I worked hard on the stories—sure. But I had luck, too." He shrugged. "The woods . . . are full of reporters who could do as good a job." In the year since the Collentine killing drew him from the woods to the docks, Johnson had written fifty stories on the waterfront. Days after winning the Pulitzer, he was back reporting that the Cunard line, following Commissioner John Murtagh's new guideline that each steamship company legally designate a public loader, had settled on Allied Stevedoring, which Johnson's readers knew was the front organization of Mickey Bowers.

CHAPTER 21

TALK OR FRY

By the late spring, anyone with an interest in the dock rackets was focused on a drama unfolding upriver in the rear death cell block of Sing Sing prison. Everyone from the lowest pier collector to Joe Ryan, the mayor, and all of the city's crime reporters knew that Johnny Dunn, as ruthless and politically connected a gangster as the waterfront had known, was threatening to sell every murderous detail to DA Frank Hogan in exchange for his life.

During the previous year, just six men had advanced all the way from their death row cells down the corridor to successfully pass through what Sing Sing inmates called the Dance Hall, reserved for final nights and last meals. Wearing the death uniform of black trousers and a white shirt, with a shaved head, each then entered the chamber itself, where he was strapped into the rubber-backed wooden chair, the prison lights dimming each time the executioner turned the rheostat dial. In the first two months of 1949, Dunn had already seen seven convicts go to the chair. Perhaps it was the

increasing disappearances from his ranks as much as the final collapse of his legal challenges that led Cockeye Dunn to buckle.
Over the months since their conviction in the murder of Anthony
Hintz, Dunn and his fellow defendants had received five stays of
execution; Dunn's last appeal, in which Andrew Sheridan absolved
the others by claiming to have planned the murder with two other
men who were now probably both dead, was rejected out of hand by
a Manhattan court as a well-worn "trick of the underworld." Johnny
Dunn broached the idea of breaking the code with a message to
Hogan.

Assistant District Attorney George Monaghan, Bill Keating's
colleague on the Dunn murder trial, visited Dunn ten times at Sing
Sing leading up to his newest execution date, in late June. The sessions were supposed to be secret, but news of Dunn's astonish-
ing crack-up leaked out, sending "chills of apprehension down
the spines of waterfront leaders, owners of steamship lines and
even certain politicians, who might possibly figure in the dock
crime picture," Mike Johnson wrote with understandable excitement. According to Monaghan, Dunn was nearly unrecognizable—
instead of the contemptuous, flinty killer who refused to testify at
his own trial, he found a prisoner so unnerved by his approaching
date in the chair that he required sedation.

Although Keating and Monaghan had worked together at his
murder trial, Dunn harbored the keener grudge against Keating,
and barred him from his cell. So Keating sent along information
drawn from his well-tended homicide files (documenting the fates
of George Keller, Tom Porter, Joseph Moran, Johnny Costello, and
others who'd stood even momentarily in Dunn's way) to help Monaghan evaluate what he heard. "I gave George a list of thirty or
thirty-five longshore murders, dating back ten years. He took it
with him on his next visit to Dunn, and made notes." When Monaghan returned to the office: "The notes indicated that Dunn was

just playing with us. The murders that he should have known about went unmentioned. The names he did give Monaghan were names he probably picked up in conversation, and most of them were inaccurate—the right murder but the wrong murderer."

Again and again Dunn promised to deliver the whole waterfront rackets setup in return for a commutation in advance. "I can make you governor," he told Monaghan. "With what I can tell you, you can turn New York inside out." Dunn wanted a deal like Brooklyn DA Bill O'Dwyer had given Abe "Kid Twist" Reles, whose cooperation led to the prosecution of the old Murder Inc. cases before his death. But Monaghan repeated that there were no promises up front without knowing the quality of the information.

In addition to clearing up thirty old murders, Dunn promised to deliver a list of paid politicians who protected the rackets. But the biggest prize he dangled was the name of his alleged boss, a mysterious master of the port called "Mr. Big." According to Keating, "Dunn had opened up to the extent of naming the harbor industrialist most powerful in affairs of the port and had hinted that this power reached into the underworld as well as into the unions and stevedoring companies."

The identity of Mr. Big was an open but fearsome secret. "His name is mentioned, though furtively, almost as often as one hears the name of Joe Ryan," Mike Johnson wrote, hinting in his series that behind much of the illicit activity on the waterfront was this power broker who held more sway than a union president or individual mobsters—a figure he could identify only euphemistically because of his influence, ability to sue, and curious lack of a criminal record, which sources told Johnson had been expunged by Mayor Jimmy Walker himself. The *Sun*'s passages about "Mr. Big" caused hot speculation away from the waterfront: He turned out to be William J. McCormack, captain of the McCormack Steamship Line, Penn Stevedoring, Sand and Gravel Corporation, and a collection of dredging, concrete, fuel, and other port businesses. A main power in the New York Shipping Association, McCormack threw his old friend Joe Ryan his yearly dinner-dance to thank Ryan for each season of peace and accommodation, and indirectly to pay tribute to his own authority. One of the many rumors Ryan fought against during his years as "lifetime president" was the story that he took his orders from McCormack.

Johnson had encountered McCormack's name early in his researches, but dared not print it. "Find out about Bill McCormack, the Mayor's pal, and you'll have a real story," a stevedoring official, Richard McGrath, had told him. "You'll have the real story, but you won't be able to print it, if you live, because you'll never be able to prove it in a thousand years." As Johnson wrote in a confidential memo to his editors in 1949, "He owns Joe Ryan and Ryan does his bidding. They lunch together frequently, almost every day, at Toots Shor's . . . There may be evidence later that McCormack also owns Mayor O'Dwyer. The Mayor confers with him and apparently defers to him. He appoints McCormack to various committees involving labor disputes," Johnson continued. "McCormack reputedly is the big secret power on the waterfront—the real boss of gangsters like John Dunn, Ed McGrath and Micky Bowers." Everyone believed it, but no one could prosecute without the testimony of a turncoat racketeer. McCormack was the real prize that Dunn could deliver.

During the spring of 1949, Hogan battled Dunn by proxy to get him to trade what he knew. If Governor Dewey granted him a commutation despite his decades of crime, Cockeye might still renege on his promise; he'd certainly done worse in his life than crossing up a prosecutor. "Talk or fry" was the message Hogan sent through the newspapers, which had now picked up the story of the Dunn watch. All this back-and-forth soon led to another negotiation offstage with Mayor O'Dwyer, who was among those watching to see what, if anything, came out of the Dunn negotiations.

Late on the afternoon of May 25, Bill O'Dwyer was seated at his city hall desk opposite a group of reporters crowding in with their last questions of the day. Everything about the exchange was sleepily familiar until O'Dwyer unexpectedly stiffened and tossed out a piece of news that sent them racing for the government telephones: "Gentlemen, I will not be a candidate for reelection as mayor in the coming election."

O'Dwyer grinned and reclined his chair as he watched the reporters scurry from the room, refusing to elaborate on his decision. He later cited health problems and a general fatigue earned during the many crises that filled his first term. O'Dwyer's retirement brought immediate crowing from enemies such as Clendenin Ryan, who'd recently nailed incriminating old grand jury pages to the door of City Hall.

Frank Hogan's was one of the names being quietly discussed among city bosses as a possible replacement for O'Dwyer as the Democratic nominee. Hogan himself was still preoccupied with breaking the Dunn stalemate, and got the three prisoners one last stay from Governor Dewey, moving the execution to July 7. Meanwhile, four more died in Sing Sing's electric chair between March and the end of June, adding to the psychic pressure on Dunn, who had now stopped talking altogether and claimed he'd made his peace with God. At the *Sun*, the latest stay from the governor and the continuing possibility of a commutation caused Ed Bartnett to request a list from his copy desk of "technically libelous parts" of all the murderous charges that would be cut if Dunn "failed to depart as scheduled" and stayed alive. After all that Mike Johnson had written about him and his gang, no one wanted to be sued by a racketeer wanting revenge.

Hogan was not out of tools. On the day before the men's scheduled execution, he managed to get a commutation for Danny Gentile, the third wheel during the Hintz killing, who'd been unarmed
in the stairwell but nevertheless got in several kicks to Hintz's face
as he lay bleeding. Gentile had started out talkative with Keating
while still held in the Tombs, then went quiet. Though his cooperation was cited by Hogan in his letter to the governor, Gentile had
not divulged much more than Dunn had in his teasing, circular discussions with prosecutors. But Hogan was gambling that Gentile's
eleventh-hour release might break Dunn's resumed silence. "Gee,"
Gentile sighed sincerely as he left death row, "what a load this is
off my mind."

The only one of the three who hadn't harmed Hintz that day in
the Grove Street hallway was the bespectacled gunman with the
jammed revolver, Andrew "Squint" Sheridan, whose later affidavit
absolving his two partners had fallen flat in court. That ruling left
Sheridan too discredited to become a witness for the DA, even if
he'd wanted to be one. Sheridan could only really be saved by his
silent boss, Dunn. Sheridan maintained a gruff front before Monaghan, as when a prison priest visited the man across the hall,
Santo Bretagna, due to be executed the next day. "What's he doing
over there?" asked Sheridan's wife. "Oh," Squint answered, "he's
just fireproofing the dago for tomorrow."

All that day of their execution the telephone lines were kept
open between Sing Sing and the governor's mansion in the hope
that Dunn might still lose his nerve. Andy Sheridan had seen his
family a last time the day before, when his wife, daughter, and a
family friend visited in the morning before breaking off to go to
lunch, but agreeing to meet again for a final goodbye in the afternoon. As the women left the cell block, though, Sheridan sent a
message to the warden to lock them out and allow no more visitors.
"We were smiling, and I want our good-by to be that way."

Like Sheridan, Johnny Dunn was wearing the death uniform of shaved head, black pants, and white shirt when he had his last meal—a T-bone, pie, ice cream, and candy, finishing with a last cigar. As eleven o'clock approached, Cockeye was the first to enter the electrocution chamber, maintaining his punkish silence. Sheridan followed his boss, wearing his thick glasses into the chamber, then removing them as he approached the chair and faced a final blur.

The lights dimmed twice and they were dead.

Days after Dunn and Sheridan went to their ends, the city's Democratic leaders voted 3 to 2 to propose Hogan as their new nominee. "Frank Hogan asked me if I would support him, and I thought it would be good if he were elected mayor," Bill O'Dwyer recalled. Manhattan leader Hugo Rogers had resisted the substitution, but heard O'Dwyer say in arguing for Hogan that morning of July 11, "Under no circumstance will I be a candidate." By that afternoon, however, Hogan had found everything had been up-ended: "O'Dwyer did a complete switch," he later told the *Journal-American*. "He denounced all the three leaders who had come out for me. One of those—Rogers—was a man to whom he had devoted more than an hour that very morning persuading to come out for me."

O'Dwyer's account was less sinister and more passive than the Machiavellian explanations by others. The county leaders had "sensed weakness in my resolve" about reentering the race, O'Dwyer remembered, and "in further meetings . . . they became aware of my [conflicted] feelings." Frank Hogan did not know every secret Johnny Dunn had taken with him, but he knew enough of them to alarm politicians with West Side waterfront connections. William J. McCormack came to see O'Dwyer twice during his hiatus from the race, on behalf of his "Draft O'Dwyer" committee.

On the day after Dunn's electrocution, the mayor hinted to visiting labor leaders that he would "consider" their demand that he run again; three days later, he announced he was inclined to re-enter the race, after two months out of it, if only to rescue his town from Tammany: "It was only when it became apparent that Tammany Hall was conniving to gain control of the city and its resources that my course became clear and compelling," he said. "I deem it my duty in the best interests of the city to run for re-election. I specifically reject the support of the sinister elements in Tammany Hall." Some suggested O'Dwyer's strategy had all along been to bring Tammany to heel, removing himself from the race and then making Tammany leaders beg for his stabilizing return.

"He double-crossed me," recalled Hogan, who returned—slightly stunned from his half-day as presumptive candidate—to fighting criminals. Only one observer tried to tie O'Dwyer's actions directly to the chronology leading up to Dunn's execution. Norman Thomas, the Socialist Party chairman who'd made H. L. Mencken's favorite speech of the recent presidential season, announced in October 1949 a "timetable" of O'Dwyer's decision making about the race as compared with Dunn's execution schedule. With a nod to stories about "a prominent and respected businessman" who "is really overlord of waterfront activities," Thomas declared, "Thirty unsolved murders on the waterfront are not the work of fate, beyond the power of a great city to control . . . What has become of the Police Department's investigation of the waterfront and its crime?"

Thomas drew no public answer, except appreciation from Mike Johnson. Without mentioning Dunn, Mr. Big, or even his own docks investigation that fall, O'Dwyer won the second term he had cagily declined.

CHAPTER 22

LAST ROUND

Each day began on Mr. Speed's side of the city room, where the old editor settled into his northeast corner seat around eight, handsomely white-headed and bent over copy. By the time the market edition had gone to the trucks and the evening shift drifted in, the last of the day glowed through the *Sun* emblems on the southern windows facing City Hall Park. Then Keats Speed would dismiss himself with his gentlemanly air and head home to Park Avenue and his wife.

Speed's "mistering" of colleagues was part of his old-school charm; after two decades together, he still called his star reporter Mr. Johnson. He could also mystify colleagues with antique phrases, once gently telling a female columnist that her "balmoral" was showing. But despite his reserved manner, Speed's staff planned a surprise dinner in his honor at the 21 Club in December 1949. Whatever Speed normally thought of big sentimental displays, he also carried a painful secret with him into the dining room that night. Looking around at the faces of his newspaper family, the guest of honor broke down and "almost collapsed," Mike Johnson later wrote. "Tears streamed down his cheeks and he was visibly shaken when he entered the dining room. What was intended to be a happy evening for him became one of heartbreak."

Mr. Speed reluctantly took his seat at the table of honor and watched his city editor, Ed Bartnett, who was burdened with the same secret, present the gift from his staff. The *Sun* hands looking on proudly all knew the fatal rumors about their paper's future, and suspected only that the warmth of the occasion had undone their boss. But even as Bart and the sportswriter Grantland Rice saluted him, Speed knew that almost every person in the room but the waiters would soon be out of a job.

Led by the departure of some big-chain advertisers, ad lines at the *Sun* had dropped by over a million and a half in a year, while circulation had stalled at eighth among Manhattan's nine dailies. But there were subtler signs of the paper's declining health. Early in 1949, Les Woodcock, a young war veteran and copyboy attending Columbia at night, knew he was due for promotion to reporter when the next job opened. His boss knew it, too. "One day Mr. Bartnett came over to me and said, 'You'd be better off going somewhere else. If you've noticed, when someone leaves, we don't replace them.' " Grateful for the tip, Woodcock escaped to *Time*.

Late that fall of 1949, the reporter Millie Falk (whom Mike Johnson had named "Miss Millie" and who had since become Millie Branham) was pregnant with her first child and puzzled by the uncharacteristic reaction of Keats Speed, who insisted she stay on until the following January. "He'd say, 'Oh no, you can't leave; we really need you on rewrite. You won't have to go out on stories.' I'm positive that what was in his mind was if I left I'd miss out on whatever severance payment they received at the end." At the company Christmas party, a week away from finally leaving her job for bed rest, she heard the publisher, Thomas Dewart, address the continuing rumors that the *Sun* would be sold: "Yes, it will be sold tomorrow, for a nickel, on every street corner in New York." He stayed with that line, Miss Millie remembered, right to the end.

On the morning of January 3, 1950, Mike Johnson got a call at home from Ed Bartnett, who had dispatched him on so many missions through the years. But even considering the early hour, Bart sounded oddly cryptic and tense, asking Mike to "try to get in as early as you can" because "Mister Speed has a special assignment for you." Beyond that, Bart added, "I can't tell you any more, but it's a tough one."

By the time Johnson got to work he discovered that, rather than surveying the city room from his corner desk, Speed was waiting for him in his private office, which he used mainly for meetings requiring some discretion. The old editor was crisply dressed as usual in a dark striped suit, but he "looked at me with red-rimmed eyes and said in a distraught voice, 'Mister Johnson, I must take you into my confidence. We are being sold today and I am an absolute wreck.'" The *World-Telegram* had bought the *Sun*'s name and circulation list and "goodwill"; the rest would be scrapped or let go. (The deal had been struck on December 1, but its announcement delayed until after Christmas.) Speed instructed Johnson to lock himself in the empty office of the antiques columnist and write the obituary of the 116-year-old newspaper where he'd worked since 1928. "I was to work secretly and talk to no one," he later wrote. Johnson stealthily took what he needed from the clippings morgue without alerting the suspicions of its archivist, Eddie Seaver. Then he closed himself in the borrowed office with a copy of the book that had first inspired him in college, *The Story of the Sun*, and wrote the saddest story of his career. When he was done, he gave it to Ed Bartnett, who asked if Johnson wanted his name attached to the piece. "No *Sun* man would want a byline on that story," he answered. When he read it, Keats Speed cried.

The following morning, Joe Goldstein came to work early for his job as clerk in the Sports Department, where he'd started during the war as a part-time slip boy tearing news from the Teletype machine. On January 4, 1950, he wandered into the composing room, the fiercely lighted place where finished copy arrived in gusts through the system of pneumatic tubes. Under the fluorescent lights that gave people's faces a bluish cast, he saw the ugly rumor finally confirmed in type. "They were making something up . . . I saw them set into the block type, 'The Sun Is Sold,' so I told that to Jim Kahn in the Sports Department. He said, 'Of course you're kidding, Joseph.' I said, 'No, I saw it being set.' " Goldstein saw the ready headline at roughly 7:30 in the morning; then, with his boss's blessing, "I put on my hat and coat, my scarf which my mother made for me, and went out and got a job immediately. I had a widowed mother and needed to work."

When Bill Heinz's train reached Grand Central from Stamford that morning, the bad news had escaped the Sun Building and the deathwatch was over. Heinz's rise at the paper from copyboy to sportswriter had been highlighted one recent day as he returned from lunch when a news truck with "Read W. C. Heinz on Sports" plastered on its side nearly ran him down. But this January morning, Heinz recalled in *Life* magazine, he was crossing the great marble floor of Grand Central when one of the thousands of hurrying figures in long coats turned out to be a man he hadn't seen in a decade. The two traded news before the old friend asked him who he wrote for.

"I write for the *Sun*, a sports column," I said.

"You used to write for the *Sun*," the friend said. "You don't anymore."

"That?" I said, smiling. "That's the same old rumor."

"It isn't the same old rumor now," my friend said. "It's on all the newsstands."

It certainly was, announced by the *Sun* itself across eight columns. When Heinz reached the city room minutes later he saw the distressed Mr. Speed and Ed Bartnett, to whom he owed everything, attending to the walking wounded of the staff, and Mike Johnson, who had already spent a lonely day composing the paper's obituary, shoring up others who'd just gotten the news. "I came in today at seven-thirty," Johnson told Heinz:

All the poor guys on the copy desk were working away like they always had. At 8:15 Bart called a copy boy and gave him the notice and told him to pin it on the bulletin board. I watched the boy walk across the city room and pin it up. Then I said, "Go over and read it, boys; this is it." They did and they were numb. It was an hour before the bitterness started to come out . . .

The bitterness wasn't soothed by the publisher's note that ran beside Johnson's unsigned account, in which Thomas Dewart blamed the *Sun*'s financial straits on excessive union demands and paper costs—burdens also felt by the eight surviving dailies—and not on the flight of big advertisers or the paper's sliding circulation numbers.

Joan O'Sullivan had come into the city room seven years earlier, as a sixteen-year-old who blushed easily, a copygirl who became the "pet of the office" and the object of much paternal flirting from the older writers. Her first submitted news story followed the neighborhood drama around a treed cat in the leafy Riverdale section of the Bronx where she lived. Knowing that "animal stories always got in the paper," she wrote up the cat story and placed it "with some trepidation" on the desk of Mr. Bartnett, who "looked like he never picked it up, but he did because he got Mike Johnson to check the facts, and to do the follow-up story." The reporter who'd covered the Lindbergh trial grumbled a little but called around for the latest on the stranded kitty. "It wasn't exactly one of his better assign-ments." O'Sullivan laughed. "I've forgot how they got the damn cat down."

Seven years after her debut with the cat story, O'Sullivan was a feature writer for the women's page, standing with the others crowded before a stunning newsroom note. "I came into work and everyone was gathered around the bulletin board, looking at the memo." After reading the message ("It is with very deep regret that the management announces that The Sun will cease publication after the issue of January 4, 1950") she called her friend Millie Branham, who was only three days home from the *Sun* expecting her baby. "Joan used to pester me because the baby was late," Mil-lie remembered. "I'd answer the phone and she'd say, 'Oh, forget it,' and hang up, day after day." But on this day Joan stayed on the line with news of her own: "It was a terrible day when the paper closed. There were so many older people, and you just knew there was no place for them to go." On that final afternoon, Bill Heinz quoted one of them, an eighty-one-year-old typographer named Scotty Mitchell, who remarked after three decades at the *Sun*, "One of my friends told me that the job wouldn't be permanent. Well, I guess he was right."

As the paper's last hours ran down, its professional routines were strictly kept while people entered Keats Speed's office for their parting handshakes, emptied the suddenly useless contents of their desks, and waited for their final souvenirs to come up from the press room. Along with other outside photographers, Cornell Capa arrived to capture the wakelike end. Soon after the final edition came upstairs and everyone walked out, he followed the group of mourners who had settled in a favorite nearby tavern, the Reade Way, to drink and wait for the radio news report announcing the end of their paper. As the broadcast played, Capa took his Speed

Graphic behind the taps and shot the line of joyless faces, from
Mike Johnson to Bill Heinz and the city desk's Homer Strickler.
Back in the *Sun* city room, a *Newsweek* reporter watched a lone
copyboy clacking his grad school homework through one of the
abandoned Underwoods.

In the coming weeks and months word got around his former
staff that Mr. Speed had not abandoned his ship, even if it had been
sunk beneath him. He was still there, the man in the corner, working eight to five in the big empty room, long enough for several
ghost editions to have shipped out, and leaving when he used to,
turning his city desk over to the hard-drinking Mr. Still. "I don't
have a hobby," Speed told a reporter on the afternoon his paper
closed, and so he was here, reading the other dailies and waiting.
"I was up there one day," said Millie Branham. "He had just sort of
withdrawn to it. I could almost cry right now thinking of him sitting
there in the corner. He was helping out the people who still had
problems; he just wanted to be there in case they wanted to talk to
him." Speed was still at his desk in the summer of 1950, when the
former sports department clerk Joe Goldstein paid his own visit. "I
don't know what made me want to go back up, but I did and he was
there, just reading the papers."

On Mr. Speed's advice, Mike Johnson went to work at the
higher-paying International News Service, where he continued to
report on waterfront matters and draw fire from Joe Ryan. But he
visited his old boss several times in the months after the *Sun* was
sold. As he told his fellow journalists in the Society of Silurians, "I
climbed the dark stairway to the City Room on the second floor.
Only one light glowed, and under that light Keats Speed sat at his
desk in the corner where he had always sat. Dust was thick on the
desks and the covered, silent typewriters." Sometimes he'd find
Speed reading; other times, just "staring across the gloom." When

Johnson finally asked Speed why he still came in each day, the editor explained, "I don't have anything else to do," but "perhaps I can help *Sun* people by coming here."

Nearly six decades after the paper's last edition came up warm from the press room, the Sun Building remained, its greenish bronze clocks, saved by a neighborhood group, still greeting passersby on Broadway with the paper's old motto. You could glide upstairs by escalator and try to imagine the productive murmur of the second-floor city room, but much of the old newsroom was until recently a Chase branch, a fluorescent space set tidily with chrome tables and blue cubicles, teller windows, and corporate-paneled walls. With some effort, the bank loan officers might have leaned out over Broadway to check *Sun* time, but the northeast wall where Keats Speed once kept his desk held a set of cash machines, and a safe deposit room largely blocked up the side overlooking City Hall Park. One summer day not long ago, Joan O'Sullivan was sitting in a hospital room, following a tiring round of tests, when she lay back a minute to rest. "I closed my eyes, and there I was floating around the old city room, looking down at people I had not seen in years— Mr. Bartnett, Mr. Speed, Mr. Brown at the foreign desk. It was a lovely feeling."

Keats Speed was finally dislodged from his city room by the building's new tenants. Barely two years after his newspaper folded and his stage was finally struck, he was dead. By that time, the scandal raised by the waterfront story he had published was escalating into a series of national touring crime hearings led by Tennessee's senator Estes Kefauver. Dozens of the mobsters Mike Johnson had named in the *Sun*, such as the Mafia leader and slots king Frank Costello, were being dragged into the novel glare of televised interrogations, as was a politician who had once paid a call at Costello's home, the recent mayor of New York Bill O'Dwyer.

CHAPTER 23

A CHEAP TOWN

Racketeering depends on what you call racketeering.
JOE RYAN IN THE U.S. SENATE

The dock wars continued flaring around the harbor, their detona-
tions reported by a growing corps of journalists whose accounts
Father Corridan eagerly scissored and filed in his office cabinets at
the labor school. Following Johnson's Pulitzer, the call went out
from editors at the glossy monthlies for stories plucked from the
hard world of the docks, and, faithfully following Johnson's for-
mula, writers for *Look* and *Collier's* soon brought back their own
profiles of dock lords and grafty foremen, downcast longies and
streetwise priests. "What drives you nuts," one Hoboken docker
groused about his pier boss, "the guy's strictly a meatball. Why, he
ain't even done a real stretch in the can."

The howl Johnson's stories raised reached Hollywood, too,
and the Monticello Film Corporation bought the rights to make a
"semi-documentary" from his waterfront material only weeks after
his Pulitzer was announced; and in Washington, Estes Kefauver
pushed for the creation of a Senate investigating committee after

reading about the shocking power of "modern crimesters." By 1950 he was its chairman, soon tossing passages at witnesses from Mike Johnson's new book, *Crime on the Labor Front*, which highlighted labor gangsterism beyond Joe Ryan's piers.

One reporter who followed Johnson down to the docks was Murray Kempton, the angular young labor columnist for the *New York Post*, who was drawn from Manhattan to the North Jersey waterfront by a battle for the former territories of Charlie Yanowsky. Kempton was professorial and classically minded for a newsman, but he made an easy drinking partner; like Johnson, he was a transplanted southerner—a copyboy on Mencken's old *Baltimore Sun* who'd settled into writing about unions in New York. Although the waterfront he saw most often was the downtown stretch of Hudson overlooked by his *Post* building, Kempton went over to Hoboken in search of the Jersey longshore feud. He found a comparatively "cheap" town of fifty thousand people where "the only well-swept, regularly-painted places of public assembly . . . are its five piers." The local hoodlums "steal millions or pennies, whichever denomination is handier," he observed. "They lack even the virtue of grandeur."

The murder of Yanowsky in 1948 had destabilized the docks, and was followed the next year by the political end of Jersey City's Democratic mayor Frank Hague and his three plummy decades of patronage. The elevation of the former bootlegger Ed Florio to Yanowsky's old position as docks boss drove the Hoboken long-shoremen to march on City Hall over his bullying methods and to appeal to their president, Joe Ryan, for a fair election. Ryan, who'd spoken with feeling as toastmaster at Florio's testimonial dinner that January, threw out the men's petition against him, provoking a strike by six thousand dockworkers that was eventually put down with help from the commissioner of public safety, Michael Borelli, who'd driven liquor trucks for Florio during Prohibition. Yanowsky had been feared; Florio was resented. But as Mike Johnson described the "swarthy, heavy-jowled" new docks boss, "His political connections on one hand, and his criminal connections on the other, mark him as a man who will be hard to depose."

At this same time, a violent rivalry broke out for control of Jersey City's big ILA local 1247, the largest in the state, and for the long-secure positions of its hiring bosses, who'd lost their old protector in Hudson County, Frank Hague. Kempton found that anyone "tainted with Hagueism" was open to challenge under the new regime, even if they'd run things on the docks for years; while in Hoboken, the city's new mayor, Fred De Sapio, also needed as many jobs as his friend Ed Florio could muster. The fight escalated in the summer of 1950, when ten army grenades went missing from a Hoboken pier and Ed Florio was set upon outside the Company K by two longshoremen who clubbed him to the pavement until he begged St. Anthony for his life. As the struggle for the local evolved from work stoppages to retirements forced at gunpoint, the first of the stolen grenades turned up.

One morning in January 1951, George Donahue, who carried the title of union trustee as well as the dark prison nickname "The Rape Artist," went out to start his car. As he stepped on the starter that morning, a World War II–model grenade exploded beneath the hood, rocking two other cars on the block and spattering a neighbor's house, but somehow leaving Donahue just well enough to take a streetcar to his union office. He was dazed but uncooperative when the police found him. Only the month before, Donahue and others in Local 1247 had convinced a rival union executive, Charlie Yanowsky's brother-in-law Biffo Di Lorenzo, to leave his position by holding lighted newspapers to his feet. Di Lorenzo in turn visited a criminal friend in Sing Sing, the former Arsenal mob member Albert Alkalitis, and a few days later George Donahue's car exploded. After a subsequent visit to Alkalitis, Kempton learned, another bombing was planned. In February, as an alternative to the rising hostilities in Jersey, Joe Ryan granted a special election of officers for early March.

On March 3, 1951, George Donahue might have been in his local's Grand Street headquarters, just blocks from where the railroads met the Jersey City docks, if the bombing of his car hadn't left him skittish and discouraged. Instead, five other union men were meeting at the office that afternoon, their desks loaded with knives, homemade blackjacks, stilettos, street guns, and even a German Luger against possible invasion. Joe Ryan had denied frantic calls to postpone the special election, which was only days away, when the second stolen grenade appeared, sailing through the window just before four o'clock and shredding the forty-foot room with shrapnel.

A witness in a nearby store saw a docks character named Joseph "Beefer" Wyckoff run from the explosion to a waiting green sedan, later found blocks away, empty but for the damp sponge used to wipe down its seats. Anthony ("Tony Cheese") Marchitto, who'd become a business agent following the foot-burning of Biffo Di Lorenzo, explained to police he had luckily left the local offices fifteen minutes ahead of the bombing. "Evidently someone doesn't want the election held and evidently it is not the present officers," Joe Ryan told reporters asking about a postponement. "They were in the office going about union business. They wouldn't bomb themselves."

As things got uglier on the Jersey side, a federal crime show was out touring the country, heading inevitably toward New York. The Senate investigating committee led by Estes Kefauver—more fully, the Special Committee to Investigate Organized Crime in Interstate Commerce—opened hearings in Miami in May 1950 and moved as a road show of brief but sensational inquiries into political corruption around the country, setting up in Tampa, San Francisco, Los Angeles, Cleveland, Detroit, New Orleans, Washington, D.C., and climaxing with eight days in New York in March 1951. By the end, television would make unlikely stars of several of the committee's members, particularly the tall, plainspoken Kefauver and his diminutive gray-haired counterpart, New Hampshire's Republican senator Charles Tobey, whose flights of scripture and occasional bouts of public weeping were a long way from the antisocial world of the sharp subpoenaed hoods before him. Tobey quieted the hearings one afternoon by urging a "return by men to the Master of Men" and quoting through a choked voice, "Solution there is none, save in the heart of Christ alone."

In early 1951, after months of its traveling national hearings, summonses went out to Ed Florio, Meyer Lansky, and Joe Adonis for the crime committee's New York event. Albert Anastasia and his brother Anthony were served after answering a telegram; the businesslike Frank Costello accepted his summons cleanly through his lawyer; while Joe Ryan got his papers on his return from vacation. The hearings were now loaded with enough Mob principals to draw an unprecedented national audience. Watching daytime television, wrote one editorialist, had become mixed together with civic duty.

One of the crime show's expected stars, the city's former mayor Bill O'Dwyer, found himself a few thousand miles to the south, living the lush life of an exile in Mexico City but preparing to return north to meet the senators as a "friendly" witness. By mid-March, two weeks after a bomb demolished the offices of a Jersey City local, O'Dwyer was flying home to LaGuardia Field, looking forward to clearing up some misunderstandings for the senators and cleaning the tarnish off his former life.

CHAPTER 24

THE CRIME SHOW

The ambassadorship to Mexico had come at a good time for Bill O'Dwyer. After briefly refusing to run again for mayor, he was reelected in the fall of 1949, only to be edged out of the job a year later by a breathtaking bookmaking scandal. A master bookie named Harry Gross claimed his operation was worth $20 million and enjoyed the paid protection of hundreds of Brooklyn police. O'Dwyer had weathered enormous strikes, poor health, and the death of his wife in his hectic first term before he went to Mexico on behalf of Harry Truman, whom he called "My favorite American of all time." He embraced his working exile as ambassador, a tanned, silver-haired statesman from the north, giving international parties at the embassy and polishing up his once-fluent Spanish from his seminary days in Salamanca.

He arrived back in New York in March 1951, disappointed at the slim crowd that greeted his plane. A parade had sent him off to Mexico, and "the feelings of warmth and applause with which I had left New York were now replaced by the unsmiling faces of the newsmen, all of them a bit tense . . ." But in his hands was a redeeming opening statement that would walk the senators through the criminal history of his city from Prohibition to the growth of the modern syndicate, as seen by Bill-O from Brooklyn patrolman to mayor.

His appearance would be linked with that of Frank Costello, with whom he had notoriously met at least once, in the mobster's Central Park West apartment during the war, as part of an army fraud investigation or as a bit of Tammany fund-raising for his mayoral campaign, or both, depending on the source. Costello would testify first, as thirty million people watched.

Costello's cumulative influence as a Mob leader ("Prime Minister of the Underworld," newspapers insisted), Tammany fixer, and slots tycoon had put him on the cover of both *Time* and *Newsweek*. (Incredulous at press stories of his criminal prowess, Costello asked, "Who do they think I am? *Superman?*") It's difficult to imagine the horror with which normally secretive Mob figures must have viewed discussing their enterprises on the national airwaves. Many of Costello's acquaintances arrived in the federal court armed with an unfamiliar new legal phrase, which they stuck with like a lucky number: "I refuse to answer on the grounds that it may tend to incriminate or degrade me." Many hoodlums balked at degrading themselves, so much so that after one gambler had refused for the umpteenth time, Senator Tobey lashed out, "Why don't you have a little sign painted and hold it up and save your voice?"

Instead of his usual routine, doing business at the Waldorf barbershop or the Hotel Madison or on the golf course, Costello sat appalled in a Midtown saloon watching the first day's proceedings. As the then most-watched event ever televised, the Manhattan hearings closed down much of American life—gathering strangers around sets in restaurants and bars and emptying movie theaters (except those that desperately advertised TV coverage). In New York alone, nearly 70 percent of sets were on, and volunteers captivated by testifying hoods skipped so many shifts that Kefauver was obliged during one hearing to call thirty-five thousand Brooklyn women back to their Red Cross fund-raising drive.

For his own turn under the lights, Costello insisted that the television cameras interfered with his right to confer with his lawyer, that pictures of these discussions would appear conspiratorial to viewers. A compromise was struck by which he would be shown only from the neck down, but this led to an even more sinister picture: viewers saw Costello's nervous hands perform a shifty puppet show instead, fidgeting guiltily with his water glass, handkerchief, or mike stand under questioning. *Time* magazine sponsored full-day TV coverage during the New York hearings, but skirted the Costello rule by occasionally flashing its own cover painting of the mobster's head as he spoke, posed before the silver cascade from a slot machine. Worn down under the interrogation, the famously cool Costello stalked out of the hearings at one point, after hoarsely demanding, "Am I charged with anything?" only to return under threat of contempt.

Bill O'Dwyer appeared before the committee at Foley Square on March 19 and spoke from notes for an hour. Although testifying voluntarily, O'Dwyer felt he knew enough about legal stagecraft to guard against Costello's mistakes. He guessed the hot television lights were designed to make him uncomfortable, to tempt him to wipe his sweat as if "the subject matter rather than the heat [were] causing the discomfort." Costello had insisted he not be shown talking with his lawyer; O'Dwyer chose instead to go in alone, to avoid even the "appearance of counsel in the room."

O'Dwyer faced a political reckoning from the committee, airing many old charges against him, including his "laxity" in letting

Albert Anastasia slip away during the Murder Inc. investigations. When Charles Tobey charged that O'Dwyer's star Murder Inc. witness, Abe Reles, had been thrown rather than fell from his Coney Island hotel room in 1941, it prompted a brand-new investigation by the current Brooklyn DA (whose grand jury reaffirmed that Reles's own poor judgment had led to his fall). When O'Dwyer was asked if he had been "embarrassed" by the unholy presence of Costello at their meeting in 1942, he gave the committee a worldly answer that might have served as a kind of motto: "Embarrassed? . . . Do you live in Manhattan? Nothing that happens in Manhattan embarrasses me." About this same infamous visit to Costello, Charles Tobey scolded, "It seems to me you should have said about Costello, 'Unclean, unclean!' and that you should have left him alone as if he were a leper."

"I had *business* with him," O'Dwyer snapped, bristling at the senator's piety:

SEN. TOBEY: Had you ever heard him [Costello] referred to as the Prime Minister of the Underworld?

O'DWYER: At that time I did not.

SEN. TOBEY: Well, we haven't a Frank Costello in New Hampshire.

O'DWYER: Well, I wonder—

SEN. TOBEY: I don't, at all. There is only one, and he reigns in New York.

O'DWYER: And I wonder who the bookmakers in Bretton Woods support for public office in New Hampshire.

SEN. TOBEY: Well, I will tell you one that they did not support, and he is talking to you now.

O'DWYER: And I can tell you that you don't know who supports you, because you sent here for money to help you in

your primaries and your election, and you got it, and you
don't know where it came from.

O'Dwyer played his risky hand, repeating a story that had "cir-
culated down here" about an organization that Tobey had allegedly
called and thanked later by form letter. Tobey fiercely denied the
arrangement, and O'Dwyer carried on:

o'dwyer: Well, I am under oath, and you aren't, sir.
sen. tobey: I will take the oath right now, if you will give it,
Mr. Chairman. I hate a four-flusher.

No swearing-in of Tobey was needed. The four-flusher apolo-
gized the next day for his outburst; there really was nothing to the
story beyond Tobey's campaign form letter, but the senator was still
so upset over O'Dwyer's smear that, as he stared out at the former
mayor from beneath his green eyeshade, his voice crackled with
indignation while O'Dwyer looked at the floor: "Hate is a terrible
thing . . . I take my inspiration from a higher source and try to forget it . . . I have lived long years and God has been good to me."

O'Dwyer's ploy had not dirtied or humbled his accuser; Bill-O
backed away and left the hearing room looking both pummeled and
disgusted.

On the last day of hearings, Albert Anastasia was invited to face
the cameras, but sent word from a Jersey hospital that he was confined with pinkeye. Instead, O'Dwyer faced an ugly surprise from a
witness named John P. Crane, head of the Uniformed Firemen's
Association, making his second appearance, who claimed to recall
giving cash bribes to O'Dwyer's former deputy fire commissioner
James Moran and to O'Dwyer himself on behalf of his firemen. In
the mayor's case, Crane had supposedly delivered ten thousand

dollars to him on the porch at Gracie Mansion in 1949, to smooth over a personal feud. O'Dwyer had no chance to return to the stand to answer the charge, but it was heard live by millions. Kefauver's yearlong hearings ended without any resulting legislation. Although Moran went to prison for extortion and O'Dwyer was never prosecuted, the damage was done.

While putting everyone in America on guard against an imported, seemingly all-powerful "Mafia," what Kefauver called "a shadowy, international criminal organization . . . so fantastic that most Americans find it hard to believe it really exists," the crime committee did not delve very far into the Mob's waterfront rackets. Watching his ILA characterized again as a club for racketeers, Joe Ryan had been anxious to have his own say before the committee. When the eight dramatic days ran out without an appearance by him, he released a letter deploring the committee's tone toward his union, especially its "grossly unfair" contention that Albert Anastasia "took over" the Brooklyn waterfront when O'Dwyer became DA.

Within months, Ryan's men would give him a last, brave shove.

Not every witness from an unsavory background drew Charles Tobey's contempt. Back in December 1950, at the end of Willie Moretti's goofily forthcoming testimony in Washington, Tobey thanked the Jersey Mob figure for his "refreshing candor" about underworld affairs. Instead of clinging to legal mantras, Moretti freely admitted to knowing everyone from Luciano to Al Capone, but insisted that his income came chiefly from gambling and his laundry business. In 1948, he explained, he recovered from a drought at the track by dabbling in political betting. "I win $10,000 on that Dewey don't win New York City by 640,000, even money." As Moretti left the committee hearing, the senators were clearly charmed, and he invited them all to look him up in Jersey anytime. "Don't forget my home in Deal if you're down the shore."

In his wallet, Moretti kept a clipping from a radio interview in which he'd quipped, "Old gamblers never die. They just fade and fade and fade." In recent years, though, Willie had been not just fading but speaking dangerously freely, an expansiveness that some of his syndicate friends attributed to a degenerative case of untreated syphilis. A decade earlier, his childhood friend and best man, Frank Costello, had sent him out of harm's way to California, where Willie made plaintive calls to Costello's tapped phone, begging to come home. In October 1951, he was days away from another appearance on the witness stand—this time before a grand jury investigating gambling rings in Bergen County. The investigation had already convicted Joe Adonis, godfather to one of Moretti's daughters, and Moretti's brother Salvatore, and fear finally overcame patience with the genial Willie.

On October 3, Moretti lost a lot of money when the New York Giants' Bobby Thomson sent the second pitch from Brooklyn's Ralph Branca on a long, low drive into the left-field stands, ending the Dodgers' year. The next day, though, as he parked his cream Packard convertible before Joe's Restaurant in Cliffside Park, Willie had marked a hopeful new bet in his *Morning Telegraph*: Auditing to place in the third race at Belmont. Inside, the restaurant was nearly empty except for several men who had been watching the windows for Moretti for some time. One of them greeted Willie on the steps when he appeared, and the group bantered briefly in Italian once he reached their table. Then, just before 11:30, as the waitress carried Willie's order through the swinging double doors into the kitchen, they shot him. One of the restaurant's owners fainted straight to the tile floor where the gambler lay dead, his pockets full of cash. The killers left two of their fedoras hanging on the wall rack, and their labels from an expensive

Brooklyn haberdasher led a deputy attorney general to size up the shooting scene: "looks much bigger than any local situation."

In fact, weeks after the shooting, Mike Johnson's friend from the Homicide Bureau, William J. Keating, was putting out a fuller version of the story: that Albert Anastasia, who now lived in nearby Fort Lee, had also been expected at the diner that day, to be executed along with Moretti, with whom he was suspected of committing some "double-cross." Anastasia had somehow been warned in time and had since earned a reprieve, so long as he left New York, claimed Keating's new organization, a privately funded group on Park Avenue called the New York City Anti-Crime Committee. In his new post, Keating was able to collect information and disseminate it far more freely to journalists than in his days with the DA. After Mike Johnson wrote that Anastasia was leaving New York for Hot Springs, Arkansas, in exchange for his life, Albert lashed out: "Only a degenerate who does not understand a man's love for his family could make up such a story," he told a reporter. "I'm going to stay right here. The committee is full of hooey. I don't care what they do to me. But there's my little children and my poor wife. God will take care of those people who talk like that."

CHAPTER 25

LEARNING THE SCORE

Practically anywhere you go among the relics of the waterfront, chances are that Budd Schulberg, who lived to be ninety-six, preceded you there. "Oh, yes, he was just here," said David Sharps, the director of the waterfront museum that floats on a barn-red old lighter at the end of Conover Street in Red Hook. "He's coming back in May for a dramatic barge reading of *On the Waterfront*." A block inland from Sharps's barge, which long ago ferried cargo cross-harbor, is Sunny's Bar, one of the few surviving places where Schulberg put in nights of research in the early fifties, downing boilermakers with dockers as he collected background for his screenplay. Except for the occasional television drowning out the bar talk, these saloons were "unchanged for generations," he wrote then, "many of them a century old, with time-polished mahogany bars, elegant brass spittoons, and brass rails that had supported the great-grandfathers of the present company." The square-shouldered men drinking fifteen-cent beers beside him resembled their ancestors, too, in their thick windbreakers and heavy shoes, and faces "weathered by sea air and drink."

The longie saloons around Sunny's have since winked out as the docks they served went quiet. So have pubs where Schulberg cribbed dialogue in Sunset Park; or along River Street in Ed Florio's Hoboken, a green window shade drawn halfway up so "wives wouldn't spot their truant husbands"; or those fronting the North River, where docker hangouts in the Village and Chelsea gave way to leather bars and art galleries and condo towers as the riverfront evolved from shuttered warehouses and rotted pilings into bike paths and sports complexes. Pier 45 at West Street, now a jag on the course of Hudson River Park, was so notorious in the forties for the Dunn gang's thefts and shakedowns that it became unrentable. Across the street, a bar and grill favored by the racket men was hit so often by rocks from bitter longies that, one regular told Schulberg, "No one would sit near the window." To the end, Schulberg kept up with the vagaries of the International Longshoremen's Association, a holdover on the remade West Side, and its white-haired international president, John Bowers, who was a reminder of the waterfront as it was before his uncle Mickey Bowers and Joe Ryan left the stage.

Schulberg began his rounds researching the waterfront by visiting the haunts of another writer. Even before he was approached to dramatize Mike Johnson's articles in 1949, Schulberg had read these daily dispatches from an "outlaw frontier" with growing fascination. "The early script focused on Mike primarily," Schulberg recalled. The plan was for an investigative thriller about a "cynical reporter" uncovering the criminal conspiracies of the docks. "At least 10 percent of everything that moved in and out of the harbor went into the pockets of these desperados," Schulberg later wrote. "What I was soon to discover, following leads from Mike Johnson, was that this seagoing treasury was in the pocket of the mob." In the first of his many drafts, the movie opens with a superimposed quote from Johnson blasting New York's hiring system and the "archaic and degrading hoax called the shape-up."

Budd's home at the time was a farmhouse in Bucks County, Pennsylvania, where he'd just finished his latest novel, *The Disenchanted*, based on what he'd seen of the last ruined days of F. Scott Fitzgerald in Hollywood. His bridge-burning first novel, *What Makes Sammy Run?*, brilliantly satirized the mogul-era movie business in which he'd grown up, forcing his father, the Paramount producer B. P. Schulberg, to defend him as "the first novelist that Hollywood has produced." They hated him nonetheless. By the time of the waterfront project, the now-bankrupt B.P., who'd once made his own silent harbor drama, *Docks of New York*, was living with Budd on the farm.

Schulberg came to see Mike Johnson just before the failure of the *Sun*. Among the most important tips the reporter gave for getting his arms around this sprawling corruption story was to seek out Father Corridan: "Go down to Xavier's and see Father John. He really knows the score." Schulberg took the advice and soon discovered that not only did the priest "know the score," but his office was filled with treasure—the wall of cabinets stuffed with clippings about every aspect of the waterfront. "The names 'n numbers of all the players," Corridan said, laughing. Father Corridan, Schulberg noted, was "a Hollywood writer's hokey dream." The two were soon drinking Heinekens over lunch at Billy the Oysterman's, and like Johnson, Schulberg found his own skepticism challenged beside Corridan's keen belief. As he burrowed further into the project, Schulberg began rooming with longshore families, becoming especially close to the men he met through Corridan, such as Arthur Browne, a veteran little battler from a West Side group of dock "insoigents."

Brownie promised to "walk" Schulberg through the hazards of

the West Side waterfront. Together they toured the docker bars of the Bowers and Dunn-McGrath territories, using a cover story should Schulberg's presence draw suspicion: the fight-savvy screenwriter posed quite naturally as a boxing manager. Brownie's reckless courage had gotten him thrown through a skylight by the racketeers on one occasion and another time beaten and dumped for dead into the winter river, only to bob up wakened by the freezing water. In the script Schulberg created, "Kayo" Dugan was a man "who had the gift of getting up." While sharing the Brownes' flat, Schulberg scooped up for his script lines Brownie routinely spouted: "Wait'll I see that bum again—I'll top him off lovely," or one he later gave Marlon Brando, "I'll take it out of their skulls."

Blocks away from the Xavier labor school, news of the movie sale and the film's prestigious new writer caught the attention of Joe Ryan, who knew that far more people might see a Hollywood crime drama set on his waterfront than had ever read the original run of Johnson's stories in the *Sun*. But another development gave Ryan the exact angle he needed to attack: word from Washington that the screenwriter Richard Collins had named Schulberg before the House Un-American Activities Committee as a former Communist. Even if he couldn't stop the film's eventual production, he might slow it down, undercut its legitimacy, and smear Johnson out of his new job as a fellow traveler.

Ryan went to the ownership of Johnson's current employer, the International News Service, writing the owner, William Randolph Hearst, Jr., a classic Ryan letter, kept years later by Johnson's son Haynes: "I understand now that the Monticello Motion Picture Corp. is contemplating producing this picture in the near future, and this Budd Schulberg has been mentioned recently by a motion picture artist . . . as definitely a member of the Communist Party."

Ryan then moved slickly from Schulberg back to the movie's hated original source:

Knowing of the long fight that your father and yourself have waged against Communism, in every form, I felt that I should call to your attention that Malcolm Johnson is employed by International News Service and while I do not expect him to change his identity, I believe he should be in accord with the policies of his employer.

Ryan closed by assuring Hearst of his sterling motive, singling out the author of more than two hundred articles about his waterfront not in the "spirit of criticism" but "just bringing the facts to your attention." Ryan's letter was passed on to the chief executive of INS, Seymour Berkson, who in turn shared it with Johnson. "Ryan is anti-Communist and as far as I am concerned that's the only good thing you can say about him," Johnson answered. "He has used his anti-Communism as a blanket defense of everything rotten in his racket union. He would have you believe that anyone who criticizes the union or his leadership is, per se, a Communist, Communist sympathizer, or tool of the Communists." Ryan was "the best friend the Commies could have because by his conduct of his union he gives the Communists real ammunition." After repeating that Ryan "heads one of the worst racket unions in the country," Johnson closed, "He's a lunkhead."

As for Schulberg, Richard Collins's HUAC testimony brought his own appearance in the spring of 1951, in which he added to the committee's list of names and explained how he'd joined the party just after college, in 1937, but that the leadership's attempts to control the content of his first novel, *What Makes Sammy Run?*, forced him to quit within three years.

When the film option lapsed with *Crime on the Waterfront* unproduced, Schulberg bought the rights to the Johnson articles and book. He had mortgaged his farm to keep going by the time he received a lucky call from Elia Kazan, the intense young director of *A Streetcar Named Desire* and *Gentleman's Agreement*, who'd seen his own waterfront project with Arthur Miller, a screenplay about Peter Panto, *The Hook*, fall apart months earlier. The powerful Harry Cohn at Columbia Pictures had shown grudging interest in Kazan and Miller's movie during their meeting in Hollywood in 1950, but as a last precaution handed the script over to his labor rep and to an FBI man for "checking." Neither of Cohn's contacts would corroborate the conspiracy of thugs Miller described as monopolizing New York piers, and one union head even threatened a projectionists' strike if *The Hook* were made as written. Cohn finally ruled the film could be made with Columbia only if Miller and Kazan agreed to some basic script changes, chiefly that the gangsters they depicted as running the union would all be made into Communists. Miller was back home near the mobby docks that had inspired his story when Kazan phoned about Columbia's conditional offer. Miller refused and, as his friend Jim Longhi remembered of the script, "He threw it in a trunk."

Kazan was looking for another project set in the east when he met with Schulberg. The two considered making a movie about the Trenton Six, a Scottsboro-like legal case of six African American men convicted by a white jury in the murder of a white shopkeeper. Then Schulberg showed Kazan his waterfront script and introduced him to Father Corridan, who gave such a typical hard-smoking, earthy performance meeting Kazan in a bar that the director at first refused to believe he could really be a priest. On-screen, Father Corridan would be perfectly evoked by Kazan's old Actors Studio friend Karl Malden, borrowing Corridan's own coat and hat during shooting to complete the transformation.

Under Kazan and Schulberg's yearlong collaboration, the reporter's story gave way to a longshoreman's story, leavened with a romance and Schulberg's lifelong passions for boxing and pigeon-racing. But it needed something else: the pithy, colorful speech of the racketeers themselves. Father Corridan told Schulberg about hearings soon convening in Manhattan, where he could see dozens of them testify, a racketeer showcase beginning in December 1952.

The New York State Crime Commission was Governor Dewey's response to the scandals unearthed by Johnson and others and to the Kefauver Committee's embarrassing invasion of his state. Schulberg attended for forty delirious days, collecting thug talk as one after another of the harbor bosses was hauled in, climaxing with the appearance of "Mr. Big," Bill McCormack—whose name was unprintable when Mike Johnson wrote about him only four years before—and McCormack's old friend Joe Ryan, gabbily defiant as ever.

CHAPTER 26

WINGS OF PURITY

*Q: Now, Mr. McCormack, you know that in newspapers and in periodicals
and so on, you've been described as "Mr. Big." You know that, don't you?
A: Yes, sir, well—*

Port Day began typically in March 1952 with a five-minute sounding of whistles around the harbor. From every kind of vessel
brightly dressed in flags came a booming tribute to the glory of New
York shipping and to men like William J. McCormack, a beefily
confident magnate of the waterfront, who gave the Port Day address
that evening at the Hotel Commodore. The year 1952 was already
unlike any other in McCormack's half-century career around the
docks, and what Big Bill felt obliged to say in his speech was quite
a departure from tradition. For the first time, he publicly acknowledged the years of rumors about an elusive and sinister harbor boss
called "Mr. Big," an almost mythical creature who, in the graphic
fables that sold newspapers, notoriously ran the port—the head
man the DA had wanted Cockeye Dunn to deliver in the run-up to
his electrocution, the criminal powerhouse whom Mike Johnson
couldn't pull all the way out of the shadows and name in print. He
soothed his audience: not only was McCormack not "Mr. Big," but

he didn't know anyone with that kind of power. A dark-suited figure with a broken, jowly profile and longish hair going white at the sides, McCormack explained that the legends about him were a product of the "man-made clouds of vilification, innuendo, and distortion thrown up by self-proclaimed experts whose knowledge on the waterfront must have been gained during a ferry ride to Staten Island."

With CBS broadcasting a secretly recorded "shape-up" over the air and *Collier's* running a profile of the once-feared Mr. Big, McCormack faced a fresh wave of experts on the ugly state of his port. At age sixty-two, he still advertised his political standing with Tammany through the yearly tribute dinners he helped put on for his boyhood friend Joe Ryan. And however deep into the underworld his authority actually reached, his sway as a power broker was sufficient for mayors to rely on him to mediate near strikes of teamsters and tugboat, subway, and brokerage workers. Big Bill took mayors to the fights, not the other way around.

McCormack had begun as a wagon boy before buying his first small fleet of meat trucks with his brother, and his influence now crisscrossed and surrounded the harbor: He controlled much of what moved and who moved it; his Penn Stevedoring Company unloaded all New York–bound freight off the Pennsylvania railroad; he held large scow, dredging, and sand and concrete companies as well as big fuel contracts with the city.

When Mayor O'Dwyer commissioned a large-scale investigation into the decline of the New York port, he put Bill McCormack and Joe Ryan together on its labor subcommittee. The two old friends devoted just four sentences of their reports to pilferage and loansharking, pronouncing their waterfront "generally satisfactory from the standpoint of the worker, the employer, the industry, and the government" weeks before Ryan's men again walked out on him in the fall of 1951. In his memo to the mayor, McCormack scorned critics who

> sit at typewriters and conjure up loansharks and petty racketeers
> skulking in remote corners of some of the city's 198 piers. . . .
> These writers, their warped minds leading them to think a fork lift
> is an Emily Post device for correct eating, suffer outlandish night-
> mares. They dream up Captain Kidd lurking in the shadows of our
> piers, plundering the Port and leaving a trail of blood in his fran-
> tic get-away.

Whether Mr. Big or Captain Kidd, Big Bill liked to call himself the "little man's Port Authority." But by 1952, a State Crime Commission convened by Governor Dewey was picking through his waterfront with a thoroughness he could not control. "Let's not be deluded into attacking the port's problems merely by seeking wings of purity," he pleaded in his Port Day address. "The problems do include the racketeers and bookmakers, but merely driving them out will not put the port back on its feet."

Unlike Kefauver, the commission chair, Joseph Proskauer, was not a senator with presidential ambitions, but rather a prominent New York lawyer and former State Supreme Court justice who suffered no fools. Even Senator Tobey now admitted that his Kefauver group had failed to dig very far into the waterfront rackets, and so the nearly seven hundred witnesses called by the Crime Commission would include pier bookmakers and racketeers, checkers and night watchmen, loan shark victims and business agents of "paper" locals who kept no accounts and held few meetings. It was all preparing the way for Mr. Big's arrival. Outrage had risen to such an extent that the five-man commission was the largest of four simultaneous probes taking on waterfront criminals from Brooklyn to Hoboken. Judge Proskauer promised an "all-out combination of all law-enforcement agencies," then added, "We are going into the damnedest investigation we have ever had."

Even before its open hearings began, the commission threw fresh accusations at the longshoremen's union, strengthening rumors that Joe Ryan, who had yet to be subpoenaed, would resign rather than testify. "Communists and their fellow travelers would be particularly pleased if I got out," Ryan snarled, taking a swipe also at revived stories that he got his directions from a puppeteer-like Mr. Big. "Bill McCormack and I are close friends and that's all," Ryan assured reporters. "I value his friendship and I hope he values mine, but to say I take orders from him is a lie." The commission, Ryan said, "will know where to find me."

In December 1952, Budd Schulberg took his seat in the county courthouse as the commission began its public hearings on waterfront corruption. For reformers such as Mike Johnson, Bill Keating, or Father Corridan, the hearings offered an affirmation, while for screenwriter Schulberg, they presented an ongoing feast of criminal detail. "It was only when I monitored those incredible hearings," Schulberg later wrote, "that I became convinced that the real waterfront was writing our [film's] ending for us." Scenes from the movie's opening death of an informer to the brothers' famous taxi ride evoked the real criminal life of the docks as told to the Crime Commission. Mr. Big inspired the offstage character Mr. Upstairs as surely as Charley the Gent's moniker came from the ILA's Joe "the Gent" Giantomasi, who specialized in breaking local dock tie-ups for cash.

"Even though the general outline has been well understood for years, it is still horrifying to be told anew that the first asset of the greatest city in the world is actually controlled by organized crime," the *Herald Tribune* editorialized during the hearings. Mike Johnson's discoveries had made people openly uncomfortable about who actually ran New York, and by 1952 it seemed their tolerance had finally been exhausted. "Business has to pay tribute to gangsters," wrote the scandalized *Herald Tribune*; "a corrupt union enjoys the profits; the powers of government and law enforcement have stood by supinely . . . All have been tolerant in the midst of prosperity, and the result is that the hoodlums and plug-uglies have taken over. Intimidation exists on every hand."

The Crime Commission leaned heavily on Johnson's exposé series, cherry-picking from it a number of useful witnesses such as his first significant informer, the ex-racketeer Dominick Genova, who had feared for his life when Johnson met him in a shabby Midtown hotel in 1948 and introduced him to *Sun* readers as "Joe."

Genova now publicly described his rise in the rackets of the Bowers gang, how he had befriended Johnny "Apples" Applegate in Sing Sing in the late thirties, and later accompanied Apples, who kept both a pigeon coop and a machine-gun nest above a West Side garage, on a night raid that netted two thousand cases of whiskey; how Bowers men used longshoremen's brass checks as alibis when they stuck up banks, and how pier loan sharks held brass paychecks as collateral. As he had told Mike Johnson, it was Genova's refusal to kill a milk truck driver who had badly cut Apple's face with a beer glass that ended his life in the rackets, leaving "a tension in the air between us," even after the milkman was eventually machine-gunned by someone else. Genova stopped getting hired at his pier and instead found work with a trucker friend from prison who, unfortunately, also knew Apples.

Budd Schulberg was surely listening closely in the courthouse to what Genova told the commission happened next, since it closely resembled what became his movie's most famous scene: the tense taxi ride shared by Charley the Gent and his subpoenaed brother, Terry Malloy. One day, Genova recalled, the trucker invited him to have dinner with his family:

> We had dinner there. And he said to me, "Listen, I've got to meet somebody over this bar and grill," he says. "Do you want to come with me?" I said, "All right." Well, we got in a cab and started to go to this bar, and suddenly he changed his mind and told the cab driver to go someplace else. When we got to this other place, he started telling me what it was all about, that he had seen "Apples" that day and "Apples" had asked him to set me up.
>
> Q: Asked him to "set you up"?
>
> A: In other words, he meant to bring me someplace where they could get at me. So he says, "Before I do anything like that—I always liked you; I want to hear your side of the story." So I told him about the milkman incident; told him why they were after me. . . . So he said, "Well, in a case like that," he says, "they told me you're marked 'lousey' up there," he says, "but I'm going to say that I missed you; that you wouldn't go with me."
>
> Well, I quit the job there and didn't have no part of him, either.
>
> Q: You haven't worked on the waterfront since that time, have you?
>
> A: No, I haven't.

In the film, moved by his brother's "It was you, Charley" speech, Charley the Gent relents and rides off alone instead of delivering Terry to his death, then turns up on a cargo hook in his camel's hair coat.

You could sit there and savor the hammy corruption. The hearings offered Schulberg many other cinematic touches: Salvatore

Camarda shrugged off the disappearance of his Brooklyn local's books, explaining, "We moved so many times, they musta got lost," while a financial secretary for Brooklyn 958 told how "mischievious" longshoremen had made off with his records. Union books went missing in forty-five of the ILA locals, including the West Side's local 824—the "Pistol Local"—and Jersey City's local 1247, whose offices had earlier been bombed with a grenade, and suffered its own nighttime break-in days before the compromised Mayor Kenny was due on the stand. Albert Anastasia's brother Jerry showed his contempt for the proceedings by spending fourteen minutes at the mike picking his nose and hawking up phlegm. Eddie McGrath refused to incriminate himself 115 times on the stand, even when asked straight out by the special counsel, Theodore Kiendl, "Now, Mr. McGrath, I would like to ask you one question. Are you in fact a racketeer, criminal, and gangster?" And Frankie Carbo, a predatory managing partner for the Mob who attached himself to well-known boxers, confirmed only his name, then went stone silent for ten minutes. After he came out of his trance and walked off, a commissioner commented, "Well, at least he's alive."

For several days, the commission showcased the Jersey waterfront of Ed Florio, its "toothpick locals" and public officials who served at the pleasure of the racketeers, such as Hoboken's mayor Fred De Sapio, who made such a muddled defense of himself in the courthouse that Judge Proskauer demanded, "And you're the mayor of Hoboken?" A representative of a Dutch flower company testified that his employer had paid $50,000 to Ed Florio's gang to smash a picket and unload $100,000 worth of tulip bulbs during a strike in Hoboken.

Another witness, a former Hoboken hiring boss named Anthony "Tony Mike" De Vincenzo, was living under continuous police watch for testifying against Ed Florio, whom he'd known since childhood but had come to wish dead. Tony Mike had lost his pier job after refusing to cooperate with "short gang" hiring scams. He had been present when Florio was beaten with lead pipes by two longshoremen in the summer of 1950, and told how one of the men, Nunzio "Wally" Aluotto, had been shot the morning he was to start work as hiring boss on a Hoboken pier. Tony Mike also explained the relationship between hiring and loan-sharking: "If you took more than a week to pay, he [the loan shark Tony Aurigemma] would see that you got to work. He'd make sure you'd go to work so that he could get his money back." The testimony of this former boxer and hiring boss gave weight to Schulberg's Terry Malloy, and Marlon Brando later based much of his performance on De Vincenzo.

December also brought the commission's unearthing of a personal history of the Panto killing. The statement by Allie "Tick Tock" Tannenbaum had been taken down days after the discovery of Panto's body in 1941, then ordered hidden in a file of the office of Brooklyn DA Bill O'Dwyer, where it sat for thirteen years. Tannenbaum's statement told of his lakeside stroll around Prospect Park with his fellow Combination thug Mendy Weiss. " 'I grabbed him and mugged him,' " Tick Tock quoted Weiss explaining,

"and when I mugged him, he started to fight and he tried to break the mug and that's when he scratched me, but he didn't get away." I said, "What was it about?" He said, "It's Panto, some guy Albert had a lot of trouble with down in the waterfront and he was threatening to get Albert into a lot of trouble. He was threatening to expose the whole thing, and the only thing Albert could do was to get rid of him."

Anastasia was at last brought before the commission, looking to *Time*'s writer like "a murderous slob in clubman's clothes." Anas-

tasia had survived the dismantling of Murder Inc. to improve himself during the war almost as much as the Brooklyn DA who left
him unpunished, Bill O'Dwyer. He came out of the service an
American citizen and a master sergeant through training army
longshoremen in Pennsylvania. With peacetime, he settled back
into Brooklyn as powerful as ever, waiting for any sign of weakness
to move against the Camardas.

For nearly an hour he put on a show, answering, with flashes of
anger and arrogance, within the tiny confines allowed by his three
other legal cases. Anastasia explained he was simply "a dress
contractor" with a manufacture in Hazleton, Pennsylvania, and
although he could not say where his income had come from during
the years 1919 to 1942, he had never controlled any Brooklyn
docks. He became testy at the mention of his brother Frank, a
priest in Italy:

A: Why should I drag an innocent name, Mr. Chairman, if I
   have a brother—that do this or other; mention my other
   brother, don't mention a priest.
Q: Well, there is no disgrace about that.
A: Well, my brother was degrade enough, disgrace enough. It's
   about time to stop it.

Anastasia was cooler when asked if he had known Peter Panto,
thoughtfully scratching what reporters called his "alibi leg," the
one he'd had a doctor examine the morning Willie Moretti was murdered, before passing on the question. When the name of one of
Panto's enemies came up—the late Emil Camarda, who'd also been
murdered—Anastasia teased the counselor Theodore Kiendl, "Do
you know who killed him?"

After several weeks' worth of docks tales, Mr. Big himself huffed his way up the cold granite steps of the county courthouse on January 29 and walked unhurriedly into the elevator to the fourth-floor hearing room. As he settled in to answer for the crimes around his "Payoff Port," he looked pouchy but distinguished in his expensive dark suit, a face that started out rather merry before questioning, less the sinister character built up by the press, despite the much-noted scar over his left eye. Rather than play the part of the docks boss, McCormack acted like the man he'd become, a Fifth Avenue tycoon who summered in Greenwich with his yacht.

McCormack batted back as many questions as he could, contesting his exact age and length of service on the waterfront, even seeming perplexed by the meaning of his own published words such as "chaos." It wasn't until the commission counsel Theodore Kiendl produced reams of crudely altered receipts that McCormack's memory began to shut down. The empire he ran from a four-story town house was too vast for anyone to keep complete track of—especially the payment vouchers that had recently burned after-hours in his Bronx warehouse. Over the last five years, some $980,000 in petty cash from four of his waterfront businesses was unaccounted for, presumably spent on "gratuities" to keep his port running. Others had testified that McCormack routinely hired scores of ex-convicts straight out of prison, and that he personally recruited one gangster in particular, the former Arsenal mob member Albert Alkalitis:

Q: Do you know Albert Alkalitis?
A: No, I do not.
Q: Never had any business dealings or any relations of any
  kind, character, or description with him; there has been
  testimony that when he was released from Sing Sing, Albert
  Alkalitis visited you at your office; that you offered him

anything he wanted on the West Side if he would stay in line with the organization. . . . That's another alcoholic's dream if there was such testimony?

A: That's right.

As they faced off on Big Bill's second day, Judge Proskauer, who had worked on former governor Al Smith's 1928 presidential campaign, asked McCormack if Smith had asked him to resign as New York state licensing commissioner for extorting $82,000 from boxing promoter Tex Rickard. McCormack denied every part of the story but the resignation. Proskauer closed by circling back to McCormack's half-century friendship with Joe Ryan:

Q: Have you visited at his home?

A: Yes.

Q: Has he visited at your home?

A: No, he has not.

But in all the years of their long and "close friendship," at the tribute dinners, evenings at Toots Shor's, or at ringside together, while McCormack admitted that Ryan had "conferred" with him "about waterfront matters from time to time," it was a one-way street.

Q: During this close friendship you never took any problems up with him?

A: Never.

Neither, in seeking advice from Big Bill, had Ryan ever mentioned the subject now at hand:

Q: Now, when he came to you with these problems of his, did he ever come to you with any problems about the existence of these criminal conditions on the waterfront in the City of New York?

A: No, he did not.

McCormack professed only the vaguest recognition of the names of well-known racketeers, even those the commission claimed had signed a silver tray in his office. As further proof of his special influence, Proskauer asked McCormack how his own dockmen could work at an hourly rate much lower than the ILA's and had not joined any of the recent longie strikes. In McCormack's last minutes on the stand, the judge focused again on the report McCormack had written with Ryan for the mayor:

COMMR. PROSKAUER: Now, I want to ask you, is there any connection between [your] report that said that all these stories about crime on the waterfront were the things you characterized as just dreams or whatever it was . . . and your desire to maintain your good relationship with Mr. Ryan and the other union people who had enabled you to go all these years without a strike?

THE WITNESS: No, sir, there was not.

COMMR. WILKINSON: That's all. You may step down.

Mr. Big had survived. He was excused looking a little diminished compared with when he'd first begun talking the day before, like a white-haired old man leaving a wake. As McCormack collected himself and left the stand, Counselor Kiendl summoned the commission's last remaining witness.

"Call Mr. Ryan."

CHAPTER 27

TWILIGHT

Q: Mr. Ryan, do you think any part of what you are now saying has anything remotely to do with any question I asked you?

A: It's got remote to do with the question of our condition of our investigation.

Months before he took the stand, the tide had already begun to turn against Ryan, ever since the twenty-five-day wildcat strike during the fall of 1951. As the walkout began that October over another of his contracts, he played his familiar part as guardian of the East Coast docks against communism: "It looks like Harry Bridges is making his last shot for control of the entire American waterfront." On October 28, Ryan had signaled that his loyal toughs were poised to crush the strikers, promising, "We'll go through them and over them, but never around them." Fearing violence, Bill Keating's New York City Anti-Crime Committee cabled Governor Dewey that night, while Father Corridan announced he'd lead a dawn public prayer with the longshoremen. After alerting the AP and his longshoremen friends, Corridan went to the West Side strike committee headquarters at six the morning after Ryan's threat: "God grant that our government may order us back to work in honor. May God protect and preserve us this day."

Bill Keating knew the worm had turned when the *Daily Mirror*, which had recently editorialized "Does Harry Bridges Run the United States of America?," reported the exhaustion of the Ryan regime ("Tyranny's Twilight") after Corridan's prayer: "Whatever happens this week, Joe Ryan is through. The terror by which he has maintained his control can never be quite so terrifying again." The strikers had demanded that the government launch a full waterfront investigation, and a board of inquiry subsequently blamed ILA leaders without fully punishing them—another loss for the anti-Ryan forces. The cause then passed to the New York State Crime Commission, the ninth waterfront investigation since Mike Johnson's series in the *Sun*. "To keep the pot bubbling," wrote Bill Keating, "I helped New York and New Jersey reporters prepare exposés of individual hoodlums who deserved attention" from the commissioners.

No doubt Ryan believed he would survive again when he followed his friend Bill McCormack into the county courthouse on January 30, 1952—ride out more bad press in his bombproof way but hang on to his power as he always had. Ryan had successfully used the "Commie question" for decades along the waterfront, an old battle tactic that had served him well in keeping his enemies off-balance. But it wasn't long after he took the stand that it became plain he could not intimidate the commissioners with his Red conspiracy talk. Like Mike Johnson, these men would call him out.

Ryan was all gregarious bluff when he arrived at the New York county courthouse, where his waterfront was being put on spectacular trial. Ryan sang "When Irish Eyes Are Smiling" on the short elevator ride up to the hearing room, then left the clutch of trailing reporters to face the judgment of the commissioners.

The weeks of public hearings had seen dramatic testimony from criminals with titles in Ryan's organization, some of whose credentials for leadership seemed to be only that they inspired fear and had made valuable friends at Sing Sing. Now the ILA president had come to Foley Square to defend his officers, with a mixture of loyalty and forgetfulness, as the commission's final witness. Settled on the stand, he took broad, even hazy responsibility for the publicized sins along his waterfront. "If the teller of a bank is guilty," he argued, "they don't hold the bank president."

His authority over the scandalous docks was wide but his details could be squinty: "I don't see there's any more crime on this waterfront than there is on any other waterfront or any other section of society, and if there is I feel that our police and our district attorney and the rest of them are well able to cope with it." The criminal records of one third of his union officers came as news to him. Asked about Harold Bowers and his West Side "Pistol Local," Ryan sneered at the nickname: "Mike Johnson wrote a scenario and called it a 'Pistol Local,' yes, sir." Neither had he known of several of the port's best-publicized payoffs. About the case of the $70,000 extorted from people seeking delivery of Eastern European furs in Newark, Ryan claimed to believe only "that our men had refused to handle the furs as a patriotic motive." Ryan was equally surprised to hear of the Christmas gift totals of his officers—men such as Ed Florio taking thousands each year from steamship and stevedore companies, sometimes insisting on shadow positions in the employer firms. Although cash gifts were "the custom" around the harbor (Ryan admitted doing it himself), he disputed the large amounts cited by the commission and denied that the practice might influence contract negotiations. Throughout the course of the hearings, all the newspapers nationwide ran the commission's alphabetical list of ILA officials and their cash gift totals, from Albert Alkalitis to the late Charlie Yanowsky.

Again and again, Ryan played the lesser evil, gangsterism, against the Red bogeyman of the docks. When asked to name a single accomplishment in "the true interests of the longshoremen" made by one of his organizers, Cockeye Dunn's partner Eddie McGrath, Ryan confidently answered, "When there were disputes we sent our organizing groups and he was down with them. I would say he was very effective in handling some of the Commies around there." The commission asked about discussions he had in 1939 with then-DA Bill O'Dwyer concerning Albert Anastasia's spreading dominance in several Brooklyn locals. Ryan had known Anastasia, it turned out, for years, "at ballgames, prizefights, the barbershop":

RYAN: He [DA O'Dwyer] told me that Albert Anastasia had taken control . . . and what was I going to do about it. . . . I went to those locals at a great personal danger to myself. At every one of those locals was a group—I don't want to bring in a question of Commies, but—

Q: If you want to bring the Commie question in, do so. Bring in everything you want.

He did. Feeling powerless to remove the charters or unsavory officials of these "Camarda" locals, Ryan had simply renamed three of them, but retained their questionable leadership (Q: "When you found the same crowd were re-elected, you did nothing about it?" Ryan: "Of course not. There was no complaints about those officers . . .").

He had a more difficult time finessing wild discrepancies found in his own books by the commission's diligent accountants. Large amounts of cash had disappeared from one of Ryan's unimpeachable sources, the ILA Journal account or "anti-Communism fund." The missing cash was spread among a variety of Ryan's mysterious causes and informants—"people I can't name." Between 1947 and 1952, he conceded, he had fought communism through a variety of means—withdrawing $31,650.81 from this special fund to pay for hats, suits, ties, insurance premiums, dental and legal fees, golf charges, real estate taxes, repairs to his Cadillac, the burial of a relative, nights at the Stork Club, and a cruise to Guatemala. "Where I spent this money from the Journal Account," Ryan explained, "I took this money from my private account to use for the Communist end of it." The "Communist end" turned out to be a deep hole:

COMMR. PROSKAUER: Mr. Ryan, we don't want to overlook anything here. We want to be fair. Does any check or any entry on the Journal Account take into consideration the Communists?

RYAN: No, sir. That was all done by cash.

Lumping all payments—outside gifts, salary, and the various accounts he shuffled money among like a private shell game— Ryan had received more than $241,000 from the ILA over five years. As he started to uselessly quibble, "Have you got in the record what I paid out of that?" he was dismissed. No government cleanup inspired by Mike Johnson's work would ever rid the New York waterfront of crime, but his long public battle with Joe Ryan was coming to an end.

EPILOGUE: SAINT PETER

I was proud to be a rat.
—ANTHONY "TONY MIKE" DE VINCENZO
I'm glad what I done—you hear me?—glad what I done!
—TERRY MALLOY

Marlon Brando came down to the wintry docks of Hoboken to try out as a longshoreman in late November 1953. For Elia Kazan, he had already played both the combustible brute Stanley Kowalski and the Mexican revolutionary leader Emiliano Zapata. Yet Brando refused the new part on first pass without even reading the script, irked at his favorite director, he claimed later, for "finking" by cooperating with the Communist hunt in Washington. The lead in Kazan's waterfront movie went briefly to a real son of Hoboken, Frank Sinatra, before producer Sam Spiegel brought Brando on board through some world-class flattering. So the film that had begun with Mike Johnson's crime series and survived attacks by Joe Ryan and rejections from nearly every major studio was about to begin filming when Brando asked screenwriter Budd Schulberg to join him for a walk. The Nebraskan movie star was ready to see if he could pass as an ordinary docker, to get comfortable in the skin of Schulberg's Terry Malloy, a longshoreman and ex-boxer whose conscience is slowly coaxed into revolt against the Mob that feeds him.

Brando was well known for his prep work. For the Terry role, he boxed at Stillman's Gym and practiced moving cargo on the docks—more lifting, in fact, than his character would have done in the easy jobs secured for him by his gangster brother. He also hung around with a group of rebel longshoremen he met through Schulberg and Kazan, particularly studying the former boxer, hiring boss, and Crime Commission witness "Tony Mike" De Vincenzo, who had turned against Ed Florio and lived to boast he was "proud to be a rat." Tony Mike's gruff evidence against the Hoboken racketeers had brought him death threats—even a gunshot fired in the Holland Tunnel. (Kazan identified with him, too, equating the ostracism he'd felt from old theater and Hollywood friends following his HUAC testimony with De Vincenzo's bravery; but no one in Hollywood had ever shot at Kazan.)

Brando proposed that he cross Hoboken in character, making a kind of casual audition before the whole city. "I told him he could never walk through Hoboken without being recognized," Schulberg wrote later in *Vanity Fair*. " 'Let's try it,' he insisted, and the next morning he met me dressed as he would be in the film, in a longshoreman's outfit with a grappling hook on his hip." "Terry" walked with Schulberg from one end of Hoboken to the other, so convincing in his checked jacket and shoulder-rolling gait that no one asked for an autograph, not even a group of Catholic schoolgirls whose rooms were no doubt filled with stashes of movie magazines. The two men managed to down beers undisturbed at one of the pubs where Schulberg had studied true Terry Malloys. Once filming began in Hoboken and Brando was surrounded by working longshoremen and real ex-fighters on the windblown piers, he somehow became even more convincing. The film was shot over thirty-five frigid days, with some dockers acting as bodyguards against local hoods who didn't appreciate the film's criminal story line.

Mike Johnson saw the tormented Brando up close one evening that winter at a screening for the excited cast. As the film ended, the dockworkers following a bloodied Terry through the big pier door as the boss shouts, "Let's go to work!" the real Brando sulked out of the screening room with his costar Karl Malden, complaining that his own performance was only "in and out, in and out." Much of the world would feel very differently, starting with the Academy of Motion Picture Arts and Sciences. *On the Waterfront* earned eight Oscars overall, including for Best Actor, Best Director, and Best Story and Screenplay. Budd Schulberg's gamble, mortgaging his Pennsylvania farm to keep his project going, had more than paid off.

It was Joe Ryan himself who first branded the waterfront drama being adapted from Mike Johnson's crime series as Communist propaganda—years before the film opened or even involved Elia Kazan as director. So a cold war argument was soon launched over *On the Waterfront*'s meanings and intentions. (Some even insisted the movie's murderous dock boss Johnny Friendly was a stand-in for Joseph Stalin. But audiences in 1954 would have known that the movie's thuggish setting was no metaphor, just as moviegoers of the Watergate era recognized every criminal reference in *All the President's Men*.)

The *New York Post*'s Murray Kempton knew something about the dock wars himself, and chose the occasion of *On the Waterfront*'s opening to honor its early inspiration, Mike Johnson: "There was passion in his pieces; their very indignation was old-fashioned because Mike Johnson is blessedly impervious to the corrosion of cynicism. To its credit, *The Sun* gave them a tremendous ride. A lot has been said and written about the New York waterfront since then; it has all been supplementary."

Beyond the academy, the film and Brando's performance even passed scrutiny with many longshoremen. "The men got a kick out of the movie," remembers Artie Piecoro, who still has the broad shoulders and thick fingers from his nearly three decades on the Brooklyn docks. "We all liked Brando and accepted him as a regular guy. I guess the Irish guys loved him even more, since he made them seem so tough." At ninety-one, Piecoro walks a mile a day, reads restlessly in politics and crime, and has a sly humor and a healthy fear of surrendering to the television. He joined his first shape in Brooklyn in the year of the Great Strike, 1951; started working steadily the next year as the Crime Commission hearings were shaking up the city; and was part of a regular gang on Red Hook piers when the Waterfront Commission was created. "Those Mob guys just believed they could do anything they want," he recalls, including pilfer coffee beans by stuffing them inside a rubber shirt until it bulged.

A half century after its premiere, Jim Longhi still saw Kazan's film as a political betrayal. Near the end of his life, Longhi was well aware how far he had come from his days doing dock injury cases as a waterfront lawyer in long-ago Red Hook. He cut an elegant, genial figure and could go from cultured conversation into one of his tales from the waterfront, where he had long ago helped Arthur Miller with his unfilmed screenplay about the life of Peter Panto.

"The hero in the story of the waterfront is the longshoremen themselves," he explained, "whereas in the movie they're a bunch of sheep. The hero of this fight was Pete Panto, but in the movie, instead of writing a story about a young labor leader, a rebel, an uneducated Jesus Christ guy who said, 'I'm gonna go out there and do it,' and said, 'You're gonna go along with this?' and they [the gangsters] said, 'Fuck you!' and they killed him. That's a hero. And who did they [Hollywood] make a hero? A punch-drunk prize-fighter who doesn't know shit . . . It's a travesty of the subject matter." (If anything might be ascribed to Elia Kazan's own experience as a government witness, it is his insistence that Terry Malloy triumphantly survive his betrayal of the racketeers. It is significant that in Budd Schulberg's novel *Waterfront*, published after the Academy Award–winning movie, Terry Malloy comes to a more Panto-like end, ice-picked and stuffed in a barrel of lime in a Jersey swamp.)

If some thought that Terry did not live up to the lost hero of the docks, one longshoreman found him entirely too close to the facts of his own life. In 1955, after *On the Waterfront* became a critical and popular hit, Brando's model for the role, "Tony Mike" De Vincenzo, sued Columbia Pictures for "invasion of privacy." De Vincenzo got an out-of-court settlement of nearly $25,000. The ever-conflicted Brando had testified for him.

By the time *On the Waterfront* premiered, the sacking of a corrupt dock boss like Johnny Friendly wasn't beyond hoping for; New Jersey's seemingly unmovable Ed Florio had recently been sent to jail for perjury. But Johnny Friendly's final warning to his men was proving just as likely: "I'll be back," he roars, bloodied, as they stream past him to work, and Mike Johnson likewise knew that no change is permanent along the docks. Ed Florio was back in nineteen months.

Joe Ryan was another story. "Racketeering depends on what you call racketeering," he would explain during yet another investigation in 1953. That same year, the American Federation of Labor's president, George Meany, finally called the ILA's racketeering by its name and expelled Ryan's union from the AFL. Ryan engineered a questionable election victory against the AFL's replacement union, then managed another close escape when Senator Charles Tobey, after calling congressional waterfront hearings and putting Ryan through another grilling, died of a heart attack. When asked by Tobey's committee about the high percentage of ILA organizers with prison records, Ryan stressed the ex-cons' usefulness in dock clashes with Communists: "Some of those fellows with the bad criminal records were pretty handy out there when we had to do it the tough way."

The movie he'd tried to quash came out in 1954, and the shape-up he'd defended so long was finally abolished. In November 1953 Ryan was forced to give up his "lifetime" post as ILA president and given a lifetime pension instead by the membership. Caught unlawfully accepting a thousand dollars per year from a stevedoring executive, Ryan did not go quietly but fought his conviction up to the U.S. Supreme Court, eventually losing in *United States v. Ryan* (1956). His sentence was ultimately suspended due to bad health.

One of the favorite pamphlets being handed around the waterfront during the late forties was an unsigned "epitaph" of Dime Joe Ryan as bitterly imagined by a labor priest:

> Here lies a man who had the greatest opportunity to build a decent union, but didn't . . . When he died he died suddenly, it was the biggest funeral the West Side ever saw. Some of the biggest people in the city turned out. People who were just as crooked and twisted as he was. . . . It's a funny thing about St. Peter. He's not impressed by newspaper clippings or double talk or big shots or flowers that corrupt quicker than an embalmed body.

The Ryan epitaph was quite popular with longshoremen, one of whom passed it on to Mike Johnson.

When in fact Ryan died in 1963, he got the predicted send-off and salute along the West Side—four hundred dockworkers along the North River "laid down their baling hooks and stopped the noisy gear of their loading and unloading machinery," *The New York Times* observed, "as the funeral car, followed by 4 flower cars and 17 limousines, passed the piers." Ryan's great friend Bill McCormack survived him by two years, to pass on his share of the harbor to his daughter. Albert Anastasia was never prosecuted for the death of Peter Panto, but died in a barber's chair at the Park Sheraton hotel in October 1957, shot by two gunmen wearing masks. Following a funeral with nervously light attendance, Anastasia was buried in Brooklyn in a beautiful hillside cemetery that overlooks his harbor.

Having devoted much of his life as a priest to the fight against waterfront gangsterism, John Corridan was heartbroken by the ILA's questionable election victory in December 1953, when the American Federation of Labor restored Ryan's old union to legitimacy. Corridan reluctantly accepted a transfer to Albany in the late fifties, and returned to teach and work his last years as a hospital chaplain in Brooklyn, where he died in 1984.

After his waterfront days, writing more than two hundred articles about the port's ugly side, Mike Johnson covered Africa for the International News Service and finished his career as a vice-president at a Manhattan public relations firm, Hill and Knowlton. But in a letter to his old newspapering friend Bob Wilder in 1970, he confessed that he would gladly have traded much of it to be back in Keats Speed's city room: "I am sure that despite all my griping about the low pay, I would still be pecking away at the *Sun* even today if it were still publishing although by this time I might very well be relegated to doing obits and nothing else, thus, in effect, starting all over again." Mike Johnson died of cancer in Middletown, Connecticut, during the summer of the Bicentennial.

Following the establishment of the bistate Waterfront Commission, men such as Artie Piecoro could finally check in at hiring halls; everyone had to register, and those with criminal records became ineligible for work. Governor Thomas Dewey, the former racket-busting Manhattan DA, announced the commission's creation with a flourish in 1953: "In establishing this commission we are deter-mined that racketeers, criminals and hoodlums be driven from the docks, together with the evil practices they spawned and on which then, thrived." The commission soon had a Brooklyn headquarters on Columbia Street, and prosecuted many top ILA officials through the years. But it became clear that the total eradication of wiseguy influence on the docks was impossible: "It's not like they wore shirts that said 'Mob' on the chest," says Piecoro. Removing guys with criminal records was easier than ending the day-to-day pilfer-age Piecoro still saw.

Seventeen years on, the *Times* reported that the commission "concedes publicly that 'there are still certain Mafia influences on the waterfront' and its members privately believe that every facet of the Brooklyn waterfront is run by organized crime." White House reports in both 1978 and 1986 concluded that the ILA was one of the "bad four" Mob-controlled unions in the country, and in 1979, Anthony Scotto, Tony Anastasio's son-in-law and ILA president, was convicted of labor racketeering. Even as containerized ship-ping moved much of the port's loading business across the har-bor to Port Newark, which had greater truck and rail access, the decades-old partnership between the union and the New York crime families survived.

In 2005, the federal government filed a massive lawsuit under the Racketeer Influenced and Corrupt Organizations Act (RICO), announcing plans to attempt to take over Joe Ryan's old union entirely. Four years later, much of the Waterfront Commission's executive staff itself was dismissed following a New York State inspector general's report that cited the "complete breakdown of the commission's audit and enforcement functions." The investigation had begun with a complaint by two decorated officers: Detective Kevin McGowan and Brian Smith, the commission's onetime police chief, became whistle-blowers against the commission's leadership over its cronyism and poor hiring practices, leading to the state investigation and both men's losing their jobs for speaking out. McGowan, who had served twenty-eight years investigating organized crime on the docks, also provided helpful background, or what he called his waterfront "genealogy lecture," to me early on for this book. The last time I was down there, the commission had a new banner on the building, advertising a special crime-tips number: "HAD ENOUGH? Theft, corruption, and orgaized crime cost the port millions of dollars and thousands of jobs."

Artie Piecoro returned a few years ago to the docks and the Red Hook neighborhood of his old pier. It was like touring an ancient and unpopular ruin—years after the decline in local dock work, but before the discovery of these abandoned open spaces by gardening centers and big chain stores, before IKEA parking lots replaced old graving docks. Piecoro found few signs left of the place where he'd spent decades of his working life. There were no ships and no shouting, of course, no loading or idling trucks; the Shaft Alley bar was gone, as was anyone who'd known him. He walked around in the spooky stillness. "Then I sat down and just about busted out crying."

By chance, a half-familiar face, another retired longshoreman who'd somehow never moved away when the ships deserted, happened along. "Finally there was one guy who knew me," Piecoro says, and the two men, far older now, looked each other over, then smiled. " 'You're from Pier 10?' 'You're Pier 11?' We had some laugh."

Budd Schulberg also went back to the docks, for a christening on a crisp October day in 2005. When he'd first read Mike Johnson's stories about this stretch of the West Village riverfront, the area had been hostage to the Dunn-McGrath gang. But on this day more than fifty years after its creation, the Waterfront Commission was dedicating a new five-hundred-horsepower patrol, the *Rev. John M. Corridan*, on what had once been part of Johnson's "waterfront jungle."

"Launch out into the deep and let down your nets," Father Pete liked to say, and at the end of the dedication ceremony the *Rev. John M. Corridan* slipped out into the river. A different city met the water's edge as the boat prowled the course of Joe Ryan's last salute, past water taxis and Chelsea driving ranges, factory condos and wrecking cranes.

On a warm night in May, I went down to Conover Street and David Sharps's waterfront barge museum, where Schulberg, then ninety-six, was expected. A repertory company, Brave New World, was putting on a floating reading of the stage version of *On the Waterfront*, and a crowd had gathered along the Red Hook pier. As the sun slid behind the cranes across the harbor, we crossed the gangway and took our seats, busying ourselves with catered sandwiches and waiting for Johnny Friendly, Terry Malloy, and their white-haired author to make their entrances.

A beggar in a black knit cap and ratty coat worked the room as we ate, having unaccountably slipped aboard to shake his cup at the captive theater crowd, who grudgingly gave out coins. Many assumed he was an uninvited old rummy, but he was actually setting the scene of the old harborfront as Mutt Murphy, Schulberg's "crippled-up old docker," who wanders through the play, the kind of character who made a soft touch of Joe Ryan on his way to work.

Our host, David Sharps, welcomed us aboard his Lehigh Valley Railroad barge, which he bought for a dollar in 1985, when he was still primarily a clown and juggler, and from whose hull he'd pumped three hundred tons of harbor sludge. The barge's restoration transformed Sharps into a maritime historian. During my earlier visit to his museum, the two of us had stood on the back and watched jellyfish mate in the noon sun, a sign of how much the harbor water had improved since the oily time when, hoping to approximate the Parisian houseboat life, Sharps first dug his half-sunk vessel from the muck.

The sun went down. Then, with the stage bookended by views of Port Newark and the Statue of Liberty, Terry Malloy appeared, holding one of his pigeons inside his jacket. He wasn't the Brando you at first expected, but he talked and moved right, and after his trick with the bird lured Eddie Doyle to his death, all the familiar thugs from the Friendly Bar were there congratulating Malloy on his con. The dead boy's father, Pop Doyle, soon turned up, dressed for the docks and almost spectral in his grief; then his innocent, outraged daughter, Edie, before Father Barry reached the murder scene. All of Budd Schulberg's characters from the old harbor were soon aboard, appearing from the gangways or hatches holding highlighted copies of his play, which they read under a hanging antique lifeboat that swung above their heads. Everyone was gathered for the production but the author. He was lying in a Long Island hospital, but he heard the crowd's applause by phone.

Red tug lights passed in the tilting dark as the play ended with Johnny Friendly fleeing ahead of the Crime Commission summons, but not before his thugs killed Terry with a baseball bat that thumped the barge's pine floor. From Red Hook, the drama would next float about the harbor, towed from Brooklyn to other spring performances at Hoboken and the West Side—all places whose dock wars echoed in Terry's story. Opening night ended with the cast going across the street to Sunny's. Like harbor ghosts coming home, or the setup to a forgotten old joke, a docker, a pier beggar, and a racketeer walked into the bar.

NOTES

ACKNOWLEDGMENTS

INDEX

NOTES

1. "DOV'È PANTO?"

7 "[I]n the course of the conversation . . .": Testimony of Marcy Protter to New York State Crime Commission, December 18, 1952. Peter Panto inspired fierce loyalty in others. Some, like Marcy Protter, fought on his behalf for decades after his murder. In 1939, Protter told this story to Brooklyn DA Bill O'Dwyer (who, after some public skepticism about the crime, promised to solve the case but privately asked Protter to get him the endorsement of his American Labor Party for mayor). By 1952, Protter was still loyally testifying, this time before the State Crime Commission, when Panto's ghost rose yet again and the testimony of Allie Tannenbaum resurfaced thirteen years after it was taken by O'Dwyer's staff. Panto remains an elusive, folkloric figure, despite the best efforts of Bill Mello ("The Legacy of Pete Panto and the Brooklyn Rank-and-File Committee," *The Italian American Review* 9, no. 1 [Spring/Summer 2002]). The *Daily Worker*'s investigative series from that summer of 1939 gives a sense of the fear among Panto's surviving longshoremen. For the background of the Brooklyn Mob and its dock rackets in the thirties and early forties, *Murder Inc.: The Story of the Syndicate*

NOTES

(New York: Farrar, Straus and Young, 1951), by Burton B. Turkus and Sid
Federis, is still the definitive source, written by an assistant DA in the Murder Inc. prosecutions and a journalist who covered them. (But, published a
year before the Crime Commission hearings, it lacks some details the hearings disclosed on the Panto murder.) I also used Meyer Berger's superb New
York collection, *The Eight Million* (New York: Simon & Schuster, 1942),
especially for period details about the Brooklyn Irish waterfront gangs.

14 " 'We had a close one the other night . . .' ": This is the account given by
Albert "Allie Tick Tock" Tannenbaum to the Brooklyn DA's office in 1941
and "lost" until it reemerged in the Crime Commission hearings on December 18, 1952. Panto's death still inspired fear along the Brooklyn waterfront
in 2001, when Joseph Sciorra was touring the Italian blocks where Panto's
funeral was held to publicize an upcoming Panto conference at Queens College. As he taped up one of his Panto flyers in a Carroll Gardens pizza parlor, an old Italian spotted the heroic portrait in Sciorra's hand. "I knew
Panto," he blurted out. "What do you wanna bring *that* up for?" "So as not
to forget," the younger man nobly answered. "But when I asked about Panto
and those times, he waved me off."

15 "Drop hooks all you longshoremen . . .": This commemorative issue of
Shape-Up is part of a boxed collection of old docker newspapers and pamphlets (#13) at New York University's Tamiment Archive/Bobst Library. The
longshoremen's newspapers trace the long-running discontent of Ryan's men
over the years—their letters' pages are often devoted to "Dime Joe" and
descriptions of his largesse ("Begorra, did ya see the tan / upon his great fat
face / His trip was paid for with our sweat / His health is by our grace").

16 "Peter Panto is waiting for you": Bals's dramatic send-off line was overheard
by the *New York Times* reporter and appears in the unsigned *Times* account
of the convictions, "Lepke and Two Aides Sentenced to Die," December 3,
1941.

2. STIRRING UP THE ANIMALS

20 "I got a story on my way here . . .": From Mike Johnson's account of his
Sun career in the *Silurian News*, the publication of the Silurian Society,
March 18, 1970. Also collected in the Silurians' *Shoeleather and Printers'*

Ink (ed. George Britt, New York: Quadrangle/The New York Times Book Company, 1974).

27 "During pauses, [his assailants] . . . asked him for the name . . .": "Hundred Floggings in Georgia County," *New York Times*, March 14, 1927. Before leaving the *Sun* to write novels and screenplays, Johnson's friend Robert Wilder published a romantic memoir of his journalistic adventures, *Out of the Blue: The Informal Diary of a Reporter* (New York: Putnam, 1943), grittily illustrated by Herbert Stein and dedicated to Wilder's boss, Edmond Bartnett. In it, Wilder describes the Lobster Trick as "the hours on an afternoon paper when nothing ever happens, the stretch which starts at three a.m. and ends at ten—a harpy, toothless ghoul sucking the marrow from the meatless bones of yesterday's news."

3. BROAD DAYLIGHT

34 "Waterfront murders were the most hopeless of cases": William J. Keating and Richard Carter, *The Man Who Rocked the Boat* (London: Victor Gollancz, 1956), p. 62. Keating's memoir of the Dunn case and its aftermath was made into the docks drama *Slaughter on Tenth Avenue*. Once he'd left Frank Hogan's Manhattan DA's office to work for the New York Anti-Crime Committee, he was prosecuted by his old boss for refusing to reveal a source, and even briefly imprisoned. Chief among the petitioners for Keating's release was Mike Johnson.

38 "We got friendly . . .": Malcolm Johnson, *Crime on the Labor Front* (New York: McGraw-Hill, 1950), p. 167.

4. JOHNNY SHOT ME

47 "In 1936 . . . me and George Keeler and Tom Porter had the loading . . .": Johnson, *Crime on the Labor Front*, p. 167.

51 "DUNN: You know you and I never had any difference in the world": This exchange was contained in the "closed case files" (#375) of the Dunn Case, Municipal Archives, New York City.

5. KING JOE

55 "We were handling pig lead . . .": Maud Russell, *Men Along the Shore* (New York: Brussel & Brussel, 1966), p. 102. In addition to dozens of newspaper articles, I consulted profiles by Meyer Berger ("Boss of the Dockwallop-pers," *New York Times*, May 14, 1944), Maurice Rosenblatt in *The Nation* (November 17 and 24, 1945), and Daniel Bell in *Fortune*, whose "The Racket-Ridden Longshoremen" appears in Bell's *The End of Ideology: On the Exhaustion of Political Ideas in the Fifties* (New York: The Free Press, 1960). Ryan stayed impressively consistent through the years, such as in his classic response to Manhattan DA Thomas Dewey's raid on Frank Savio's loan-sharking ring in 1941: "We cannot conceive of any member of our organization, especially in this port where we have so many representatives covering the waterfront daily, who would be foolish enough to pay any of his earnings to anybody, except the $20 a year dues . . ."

6. THE BIG STORY

63 "Mr. Speed, Mr. Bartnett . . .": This and many other city room memos came to me through the generosity of Haynes Johnson, and without them the evo-lution of Mike's investigation would have been very difficult to re-create. Other details of the Johnsons' life at this time also came from Haynes, espe-cially about the threatening calls to the house and Mike's reactions.

7. THEY'D NEVER KILL A REPORTER

68 "Sometimes she'd pick up the phone . . .": Descriptions of the tension at Johnson's home and the *Sun* during this time come from Haynes Johnson, Millie Branham, and what Mike Johnson himself wrote.

8. THE LEECH AND THE THUG

80 "Asked whether [William] Warren might return to . . .": Malcolm Johnson, *Crime on the Labor Front* (New York: McGraw-Hill, 1950), p. 138.

9. A LOUSY BUCK

83 "I haunted waterfront saloons . . .": Johnson, *Crime on the Labor Front*, p. 90.

86 "You want to know what's wrong with the waterfront?": Allen Raymond, *Waterfront Priest* (New York: Henry Holt & Co., 1955), p. 88. Mike first profiled Father Corridan for the *Sun*, and more expansively in 1952, for the men's magazine *Argosy*, in "Father Gangbuster," an article whose title he hated but whose prose was heartfelt. I also gained a good sense of Corridan through the collection of his papers at Fordham University.

87 "I suppose some people would smirk . . .": Raymond, *Waterfront Priest*, p. 90. The sermon Budd Schulberg later inserted into *On the Waterfront*. Corridan's book is a strangely uneven thing to read, considering the bluntness and bravery of its subject, but the long "consolidated chronology" he and Carter prepared is the real find: collected at Fordham, it contains a detailed time line of crimes and longshore disruptions around the port during Corridan's waterfront tenure, and it steered me to a number of events I'd missed. The chronology was just a taste of the famous criminal files Corridan kept in his office cabinets at the Xavier labor school.

10. A CUP OF COFFEE

94 " 'That's ridiculous!' he roared . . .": I reconstructed the showdown between Johnson and Ryan from Johnson's interview that ran in the *New York Sun* on December 7, 1948, and from portraits of Ryan taken in his office for *Life* magazine (Time Life/Getty Images).

11. MEET THE BOYS

102 "I took a nice bite out of him . . .": *Reminiscences of Cyrus Ching*, Oral History Project Office, Columbia University. All Mencken quotes in this chapter are from *Mencken's Last Campaign: H. L. Mencken on the 1948 Election*, ed. Joseph C. Goulden (Washington, D.C.: The New Republic Book Company, 1976).

NOTES

12. ABOVE THE FOLD

108 "I see where Mr. Johnson said . . .": This and other city room memos came compliments of Haynes Johnson. Quotes in this chapter from Les Woodcock are from an interview with the author, May 7, 2007.

13. JUST STRANGERS

112 "A man does not complain . . .": John Corridan, "Longshoremen's Case," *America: The National Catholic Weekly*, November 15, 1948.

14. COMMUNISTS AND NEWSMEN

117 "This sudden strike was caused by the articles of Malcolm Johnson . . .": *New York Sun*, November 10, 1948.

15. THE PEACEMAKER

124 "Senator Taft wants me to keep an eye on you": This anecdote comes to me from Jon Margolis. For more on the 1948 strikes in New York, see William Margolis's official report for the Federal Mediation and Conciliation Service (12/31/48), National Archives, and *Reminiscences of Cyrus Ching*, Oral History Project Office, Columbia University.

16. OUR WIT'S END

131 "Dunn's job was to be a watchdog . . .": Rodney Campbell, *The Luciano Project: The Secret Wartime Collaboration of the Mafia and the U.S. Navy* (New York: McGraw-Hill, 1977), p. 103.

17. TO SPEAK WITHOUT FEAR

137 "I'd learned the lesson well and was able to say . . .": Reminiscences of Paul O'Dwyer, Oral History Project Office, Columbia University. See also *Beyond the Golden Door* (New York: St. John's University Press, 1987), a collection of William O'Dwyer's writings (on his Irish boyhood, the Murder Inc. cases, the mayoral years, and his disastrous cooperation in the Kefauver hearings),

edited by Paul O'Dwyer, whose transition text reveals an appealingly loyal little brother. It was Paul who drove Bill to his grand jury proceedings in Brooklyn in 1945, when he was charged with "laxity" for not arresting Albert Anastasia for murder.

18. THE MEETING OF MINDS

143 "Mike Johnson and the New York Sun are to be congratulated . . .": Bulletin from Xavier Institute of Industrial Relations Collection/Fordham University Archives and Special Collections.

144 "I fancied myself as a reasonably hard-bitten . . .": Malcolm Johnson, "Father Gangbuster," *Argosy*, March 1952. See also Colin J. Davis's portrait of Corridan, " 'Launch out into the deep and let down your nets': Father John Corridan, S.J., and New York Longshoremen in the Post–World War II Era," *Catholic Historical Review*, January 31, 2000. Also, James Fisher, "Waterfront Priest," *Company* magazine (Summer 2003). Budd Schulberg's remembrance of "Father Pete" appears in a recent gathering of Mike Johnson's reporting, with an introduction by Haynes Johnson, *On the Waterfront: The Pulitzer Prize–Winning Articles That Inspired the Classic Movie and Transformed New York Harbor* (New York: Chamberlain Brothers/Penguin, 2005).

19. THEY KILL IN THE DARK

148 "The saloons now are hangouts . . .": Johnson, *Crime on the Labor Front*, p. 219.

20. OUT OF THE WOODS

151 "It was down near the piers that . . .": Arthur Miller, *Timebends: A Life* (New York: Grove Press, 1987), p. 146. This section is also based on interviews with Miller's friend Vincent "Jim" Longhi, who took him around the docks. When I brought up discrepancies I'd found in Miller's lyrical account of the Panto era, Longhi smiled and said, "Don't forget. It's called 'Time *Bends*.' "

21. TALK OR FRY

156 "The notes indicated that Dunn was just playing . . .": William J. Keating
and Richard Carter, *The Man Who Rocked the Boat* (London: Victor Gollancz, 1956), p. 146. Beyond the daily newspaper accounts of the run-up to
the Dunn and Sheridan executions at Sing Sing, I consulted historical
pamphlets (*Sing Sing Prison Electrocutions, 1891–1963*, by the Ossining
Historical Society), the waterfront reporting of Guy Richards in the *Herald-
American*, and Richard Rovere's profile of the Manhattan DA Frank Hogan,
"Father Hogan's Place," which ran in *The New Yorker*, August 16, 1947.

22. LAST ROUND

167 "All the poor guys on the copy desk . . .": From W. C. Heinz, "The Sun Is
Sold," *Life*, January 16, 1950. This chapter relies on interviews with former
Sun staff, as well as accounts of the last day by Johnson.

23. A CHEAP TOWN

173 "His political connections on one hand, and his criminal connections . . .":
Johnson, *Crime on the Labor Front*, p. 213.

24. THE CRIME SHOW

180 "I had *business* with him . . .": George Walsh, *Public Enemies: The Mayor,
the Mob, and the Crime That Was* (New York: W. W. Norton, 1980), p. 215.
Walsh does a terrific job following the O'Dwyer-Costello relationship and its
prominence at the Kefauver hearings. Also, the May 1951 edition of Estes
Kefauver's *Crime in America* contains some surprising mixed feelings about
the damage done to O'Dwyer.

25. LEARNING THE SCORE

188 "I understand now that . . .": Mike Johnson saved Ryan's toxic letter, and
Haynes Johnson shared it with me. This chapter also draws on Budd Schulberg's various accounts of the making of *On the Waterfront*, from a story-
behind-the-story in the *Times* in 1954, to the introduction to the published

shooting script, interviews, a letter to the *Times* in 1994 (to counter claims made in Marlon Brando's autobiography), and most recently in *Vanity Fair* ("The King Who Would Be Man," March 2005), as well as two phone conversations with the author.

26. WINGS OF PURITY

198 "We had dinner there . . .": This cinematic passage from the report of the Crime Commission is proof that Budd Schulberg kept alert during the weeks of hearings. But gritty scenes such as this can be found throughout the mammoth report.

200 "I grabbed him and mugged him . . .": *New York Herald Tribune*, "Anastasia Linked to '39 Murder in Report Read at Crime Probe," December 19, 1952.

27. TWILIGHT

205 "Q: Mr. Ryan, do you think any part of what you are now saying . . .": Report of New York State Crime Commission hearings, January 30, 1953, New York University's Tamiment Archive/Bobst Library.

28. EPILOGUE: SAINT PETER

211 "I was proud to be a rat": In addition to the period coverage of the Crime Commission hearings, I supplemented Schulberg and Kazan's memoirs with the Hoboken Historical Museum's superb booklet on the making of the movie, "*On the Waterfront*, Starring Hoboken, New Jersey," with its lead historical essay by Sada Fretz.

214 "The hero in the story . . .": Interview with the author, March 1, 2006.

ACKNOWLEDGMENTS

This book would not have been possible without the generosity of Mike Johnson's elder son, Haynes Johnson, whose patience with my many scattered queries—about his father's battles with the Klan in rural Georgia, the layout of the old *Sun* city room, or his father's reading habits or poker partners—helped lift up the story several times when it threatened to flag. The family letters he shared, as well as a crucial stash of old city room memos, helped me to understand what kind of man his father had been and to imagine how his investigation evolved. A distinguished historian himself, Haynes has always treated the past with the respect it deserves, even when, as in this case, it leads into his boyhood home. His love for his late father and for history in general were always clear from his kindness toward my long project.

I also owe a debt of thanks to Eve Berliner, editor of the *Silurian News*, a publication of the Society of the Silurians, for putting me in touch with several of Mike's surviving city room colleagues: Les Woodcock, Joe Goldstein, Joan O'Sullivan, and Millie Branham ("Miss Millie," as Mike Johnson called her). Dave Anderson, most notably of the *New York Times*, was quite helpful in remembering the *Sun* city room, where he began as a copyboy during the war. My thanks also to two scholars of the late waterfront leader Peter Panto: Joseph Sciorra of Queens

ACKNOWLEDGMENTS

College's John D. Calandra Italian American Institute, who keeps Panto's photo in his office; and the labor historian Bill Mello, a longshoreman's son himself, who shared his thesis about the waterfront labor movement and put me in touch with the retired Brooklyn longshoreman Artie Piecoro, who taught me a great deal. I would also like to thank Jon Margolis, whom I've known since long before I could take notes. I'd never known what his father, Bill Margolis, had done for a living until I accidentally spotted him pictured uneasily next to Joe Ryan in news photos of the '48 strike talks. Bill Margolis was sent by the Federal Mediation and Conciliation Service into the center of that and many other labor storms, and I thank Jon for lending me his father's clippings and his Harry Bridges stories.

I am tremendously grateful to my endlessly supportive family: my late grandfather, F. Champion Ward, whose own billiards partners toward the end of his life included a wounded veteran of Omaha Beach and a Manhattan parking garage king, once observed that "you like *characters*," and he might have seen this book as the inevitable result of happy years of character collecting. His wife, my beautiful grandmother Duira Ward, read the manuscript even while in the hospital, loyally finding something to like despite the story's rough parade of thugs. The book had been proudly brought to her by my father, Geoffrey Ward, who remains my ideal reader and lifelong friend. My profound thanks to Diane and Garrett, Jake and Kelly, and Andy for their wisdom, perspective, and humor during this long project. And to my mother, Phyllis Alden, for her love and original point of view.

Thanks also to Patrice Kane, head of Archives and Special Collections, Fordham University Library, which houses the papers of the Xavier Institute of Industrial Relations. My work greatly benefited from my knowing David Sharps, of the Waterfront Museum, who keeps the story of the working waterfront vividly alive. I am also grateful to two writers for whom gang history is anything but a guilty pleasure, the novelist Kevin Baker and the writer and Luciano expert Allen Barra (who was particularly helpful on the minutiae of criminal allegiances around the harbor). Also to *The Irish Echo*'s reporter Peter McDermot, a proven friend of the waterfront story, who was generous with his sources and phone numbers.

I consulted many docks memoirs, from *Dock Walloper* to *Waterfront Priest* and *The Man Who Rocked the Boat*, but the number of academic labor histories that touch on the waterfront is surprisingly small, including Howard Kimeldorf's excellent *Reds or Rackets? The Making of Radical and Conservative Unions on the Waterfront*; Vernon Jensen's *Strife on the Waterfront*; and Colin J. Davis's

Waterfront Revolts. An earlier priest on the waterfront, Reverend Edward E. Swanstrom, became such an effective advocate for the reform case that Joe Ryan banned him from appearing at the ILA convention to discuss his book, *The Waterfront Labor Problem: A Study in Decasualization and Unemployment Insurance* (New York: Fordham University Press, 1938). Swanstrom, who learned the docks from the Brooklyn side, offers an exhaustive portrait of the working harbor leading up to the Panto uprising. In its own category is Maud Russell's *Men Along the Shore* (1966), an alternately vexing and highly useful book that offers a defense of Joe Ryan's thuggish reign over the International Longshoremen's Association, but also contains wonderful long passages from Ryan's unpublished memoirs.

I spent many days in the basement microfilm room of New York University's Elmer Holmes Bobst Library, comparing accounts from long-defunct newspapers of periodic shutdowns and uprisings around the port, of the deaths of many docks characters (enough so that I developed my own "payback file" of retributive pier violence), and the government testimony of victims and perpetrators. But upstairs, at NYU's Tamiment Library and Robert F. Wagner Labor Archives, I found boxes of memorabilia from the International Longshoremen's Association, maritime workers' oral histories done with Sam Madell and Rev. Philip Carey, and I read the full set of transcripts of the forty-five-day New York State Crime Commission Hearings, surely the most dramatic, darkly funny, and enjoyable government publication ever printed before Watergate.

Those lost newspapers too rarified for the Bobst Collection (the *Daily Mirror*, the *New York Telegram*) I usually found at the New York Public Library, which also has, deep in the stacks beneath Bryant Park, vintage phone listings for finding old waterfront taverns or the Brooklyn cigar store from which Peter Panto's killers called him. My thanks to Columbia University for the use of its Oral History Project's *Reminiscences* by Cyrus Ching and Paul O'Dwyer; and to the Museum of Television and Radio, where I watched Frank Costello sweat, Bill O'Dwyer bristle, and "Tough Tony" Anastasio bob and weave. Lenora Gidlund, director of the city's Municipal Archives, on Chambers Street, down the block from the New York Sun Building, pointed me toward many strange discoveries— the arrest records of North River racketeers, Andy Hintz's coroner's report, and the DA's complete files from the Dunn murder case (just as Mike Johnson saw them in 1948), as well as some unsolicited treasures: sitting on a windowsill facing the Tweed Courthouse one summer's day was an open cardboard box labeled "Murder, Inc.," containing dozens of thirties mug shots and police photos

ACKNOWLEDGMENTS

of chalk-body outlines and of the crumpled form of Abe "Kid Twist" Reles, well-dressed but dead, after his mysterious fall in Coney Island.

I would especially like to thank two men who could see the book that still lay buried in the rubble of its subject matter: my loyal agent Ed Breslin, for his cheerful, inexhaustible confidence in the project, his patience and sustaining good humor, and his uncompromising belief in the importance of books and good writing; and my editor at Farrar, Straus and Giroux, Paul Elie, who, because of his own deep and varied interests, always viewed the waterfront story as merely neglected or forgotten and never as hopelessly obscure. This book took far longer than its author promised, but Paul saw it patiently into the office and continued to champion it, despite a radically changed publishing environment. I am honored to have him as my editor.

Finally, my thanks to three witnesses to this story who passed away before I could show them a finished book:

Vincent "Jim" Longhi, in addition to being a fabulous storyteller, helped me to understand the fearful climate of the late thirties and early forties along the docks, especially the time of the Panto rebellion against the racketeers.

Though I knew him only on the phone, Budd Schulberg never moved entirely away from the harbor in his imagination, luckily for me, even six decades after writing *On the Waterfront*. He clearly had invested more of himself in it during those five years around the docks than in any other project, and by the end of my own stint, I could understand its haunting effect.

The third loss was my friend the great sportswriter W. C. Heinz, whom I knew from doing boxing writing, but who was originally a copyboy, war correspondent, and sports columnist at the *Sun*. One day on the phone, Bill walked me through the 1940s city room as if I were the new guy trailing along through his first-day introductions. We climbed the stairs and greeted the long-gone Mr. Chandler at the door and crossed the newsroom floor, noting the distinguished line of editors bent to their copy, before Bill finally left me for his own remembered seat back in sports. I hope it would please Heinz just a little to have the old *Sun* hands back at their desks.